World Sound Matters

Jonathan Stock

TRANSCRIPTIONS

ED 12571

SCHOTT
EDUCATIONAL PUBLICATIONS

Mainz · London · Berlin · Madrid · New York · Paris · Prague · Tokyo · Toronto

Contents

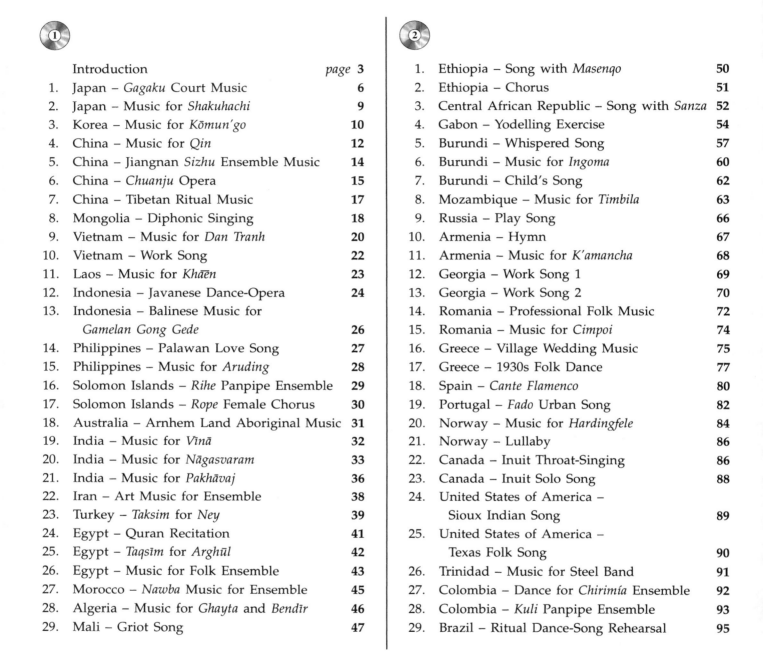

The author and publisher would like to thank Peter Nickol and Paul Terry for their invaluable assistance in preparing this project for publication

British Library Cataloguing-in-Publication Data. A catalogue record of this book is available from the British Library

ED 12571 ISBN 0 946535 81 7

Typeset by Musonix Typesetting
Cover design by Bob Linney
Printed in England by Hobbs the Printers Ltd, Totton, Hampshire SO40 3YS

Introduction

Overview

World Sound Matters is a fully-integrated anthology of music from around the world, consisting of:

- 2 compact discs of 58 traditional music recordings, representing 35 different countries
- notated transcriptions of each recorded example
- explanatory texts covering the special context of each style and its musical content
- 2 sets of progressive pupil listening-based questions for each musical style

Each unit is free-standing and can be effectively used on its own. Alternatively, multiple units can be combined, in any order, to provide an introduction to the musical traditions of the world.

The music incorporated in *World Sound Matters* has been carefully selected and prepared by an ethnomusicologist in consultation with other music specialists and professionals actively engaged in music education. Two aims have been paramount: on the one hand, readers need analyses of a wide range of musical traditions which are both authoritative and yet remain accessible to the non-specialist; on the other hand, the many musicians whose work appears on the sound recordings deserve a thorough and sympathetic study which neither cheapens nor dilutes their artistry.

The anthology of transcriptions

Although ethnomusicologists are trained to write down musical sound in visual symbols, we rely on contextual knowledge of the music as much as on our ears. Knowing how an instrument works, how its strings are tuned, what its performance techniques are and what the local music theory admits as acceptable greatly assists the process of converting musical sounds to graphic signs. However, this familiarity is not easily acquired, and there are probably few ethnomusicologists with intimate knowledge of more than three or four different musical traditions. Sometimes, specialists in the music of other cultures helped by contributing transcriptions and notes, and a handful of my bolder students at the University of Durham gave of their best efforts. Nonetheless, it was not always possible to find someone with both the requisite local knowledge and the free time to undertake each transcription, and most of them I completed myself. The further I moved from familiar territory, which in my case means Chinese traditional music and Western classical music, the harder it was to find ways to write down what I thought I heard.

The phrase 'thought I heard' is important, because the human ear and mind are closely linked. Hearing music is not a passive process of taking in sound waves. It involves perception, or the making sense of the sounds, which is where experience and training come in. This means that a transcriber has no choice but to rationalize each set of sounds to his or her own ways of thinking about music. I may have detected patterns where the originators of the music would say that none exist, and I may have thought I heard intervals or rhythms which are not quite those so carefully performed by the musicians. Of course, I have very probably made straightforward errors too, but the point of explaining all this is to stress that musical perception is quite an individual quality and one greatly reliant upon a listener's experience. Given this variable, written transcriptions of musical sounds, however accurate, will never be able to tell the whole story. The sound recordings should, of course, be taken as authoritative, and the transcriptions as subsequent attempts to describe them in writing. They are thus quite unlike the scores of Western musical works, where the symbols typically prescribe a series of notes which, when realized adequately by the performer, should result in the sounds the composer had in mind.

Despite all this, written transcriptions are extremely convenient tools, allowing the viewer to take in a whole piece in one glance, or to compare, outside of the passage of performance time, different passages. In general, the transcriptions in this collection employ stave notation. Stave notation has the advantages of being both widely understood and a very condensed means of writing down certain musical information. It is strong on pitch and rhythm, which are graphically laid out on the vertical and horizontal axes respectively. It is less strong on attributes such as timbre or microtonal adjustment of existing notes, aspects which are very important in some musical traditions. For reasons such as these, the stave notation employed is typically adapted in some way, for instance an adjusted key signature or layout, to better suit the facts of the music in question. Special symbols are explained in each case, and additional comments to guide the viewer are found on every transcription.

The transcriptions are designed primarily for use with the sound recordings. A few, especially the unaccompanied songs, are suitable without further adaptation for use as performance scores. Even in these cases, though, I would still recommend learning the songs by ear from the recording and using the transcription as a supplementary guide. Another role of the transcriptions might be to act as models for pupils' own project work. In many music curricula it is possible for a pupil to complete a special extended study. Partial transcriptions could be continued by students equipped with the original CD. Or, taking the transcription and its accompanying notes as a model, they could perhaps study an alternative track from the same recording.

A further possible use of these transcriptions is as a resource for composers. By this I mean not so much imitating the sounds of different musical traditions, although one could perhaps have fun doing that. Instead, close study of the ways in which different people from around the world combine musical sounds and structure musical passages will suggest musical techniques to those who are interested in structuring sounds in their own musical idioms. For reasons of focus, this line of thought is not pursued much further in this anthology, but the imaginative reader will find much scope here for fruitful experimentation.

facing page: **World Map showing where the music in this anthology originated**

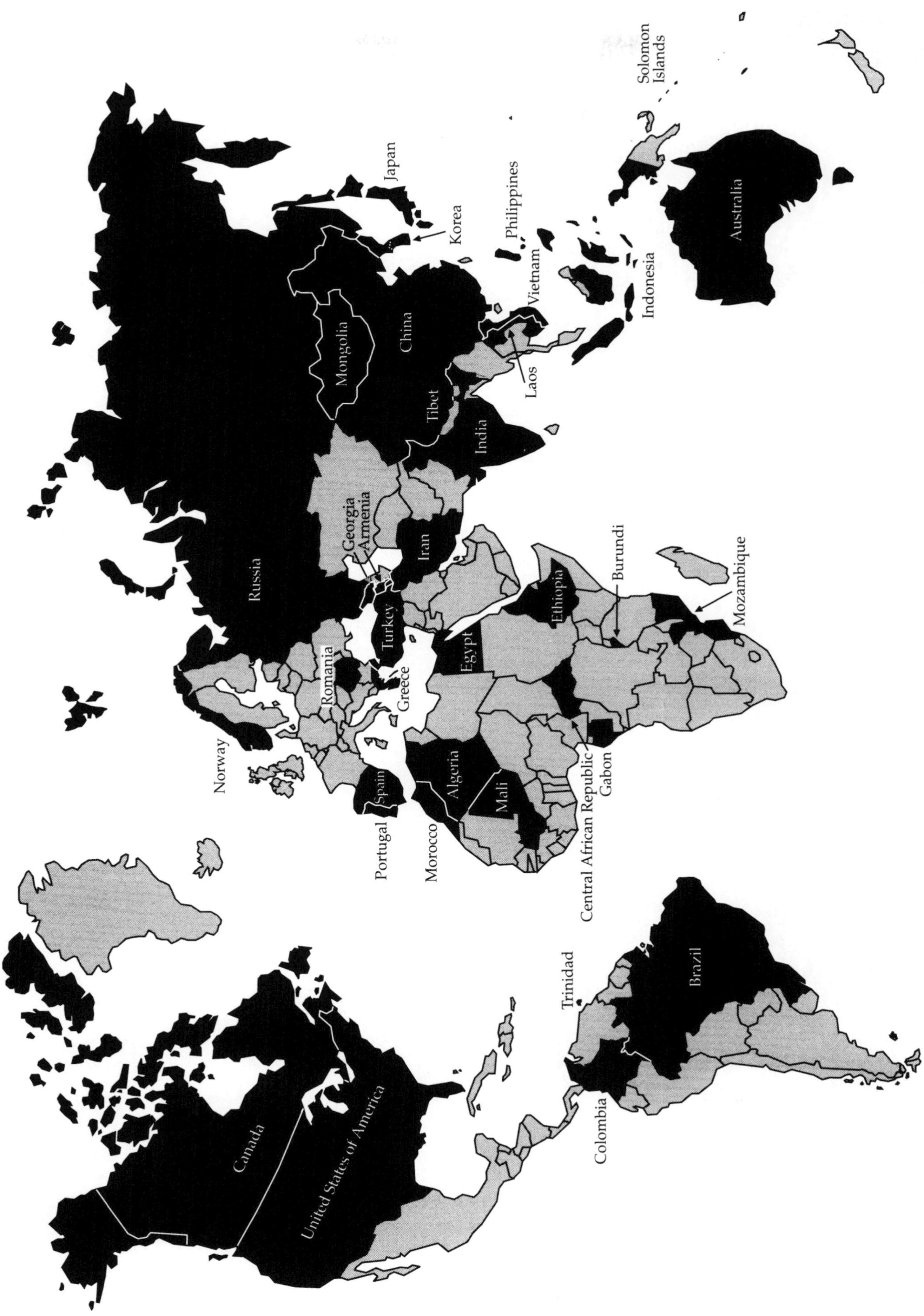

Canada
United States of America
Colombia
Trinidad
Brazil
Portugal
Morocco
Spain
Algeria
Mali
Central African Republic
Gabon
Norway
Romania
Greece
Turkey
Egypt
Ethiopia
Burundi
Mozambique
Georgia
Armenia
Iran
Russia
India
Tibet
Mongolia
China
Laos
Vietnam
Korea
Japan
Philippines
Indonesia
Australia
Solomon Islands

Japan

1. *Gagaku* Court Music: Etenraku

♩ = **c.33** *(with a gradual accel. to c.38 by the end of this extract)*

(1 player only)
Ryūteki
Hichiriki
Shō
Keko
(gradual accel.)
Taiko
Shōko
Sō
Biwa

5
6
6
p

(all)
10
(cluster chord)
(cluster chord)
(cluster chord)
(cluster chord)
(cluster chord)
(cluster chord)

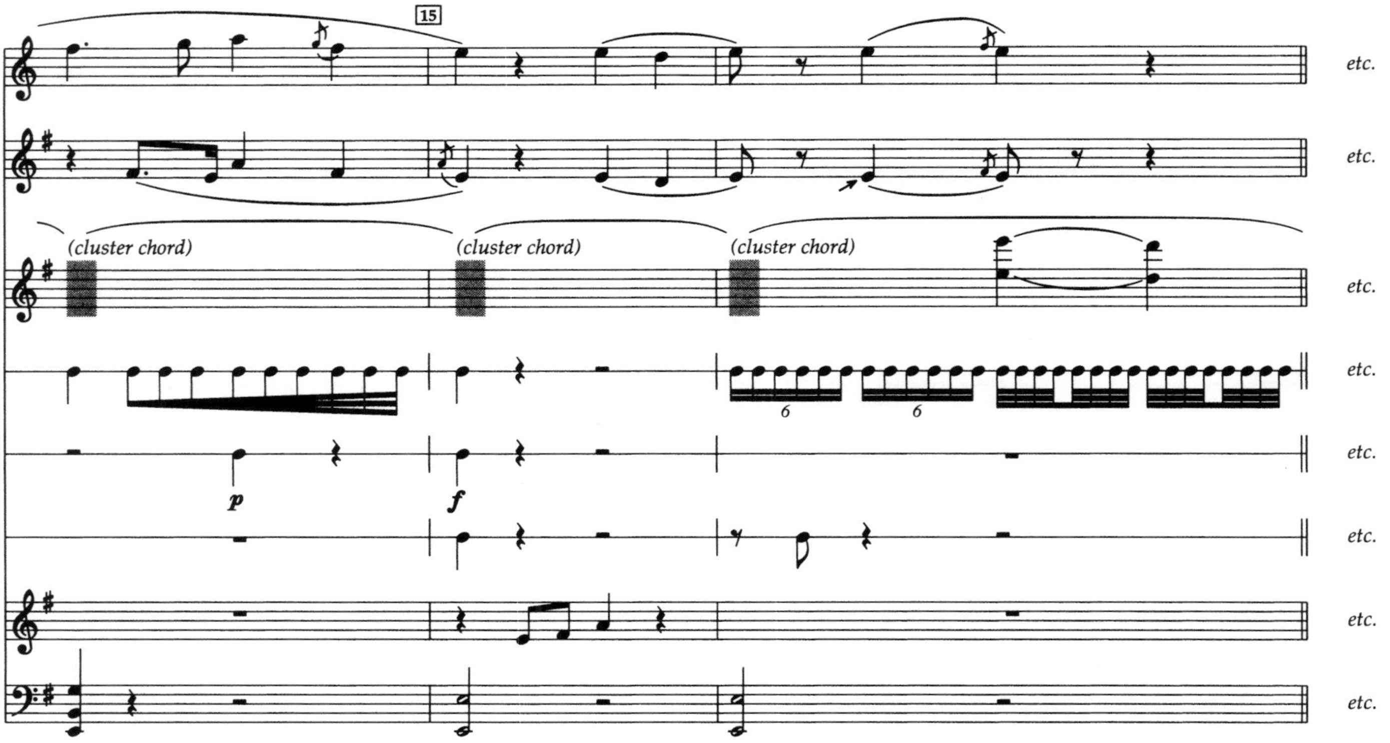
15
(cluster chord)
(cluster chord)
(cluster chord)
6
6
p
f
etc.

Transcription Notes

This is a selective, highlight transcription of section A

The 4th beats are generally expanded in tempo

↗ slide in direction indicated

The biwa chords are spread from high to low

2. Music for *Shakuhachi*: Kokū

♩ = c.60 (but quite flexible)
Shakuhachi
10
20
30
40
50
etc.

Transcription Notes

Transcribed one semitone above the recorded pitch

↗ glissando (pitch slide) in direction indicated

* breath attack with air blown audibly across the surface of the blowing edge

3. Music for *Komun'go*: Sanjo in kyemyonjo mode

= c.60
Kōmun'go
Changgo
5

10
etc.

Transcription Notes

Transcribed one semitone above the recorded pitch

The accents in the kōmun'go part show where the plectrum strikes the instrument; slurred notes all result from the same pluck

⌝ curved lines show pitch slides;

~~~~ vibrato

⌇ octave performed from low to high

ʌ higher grace note followed by immediate drop to main note

Open (left hand) changgo notes are notated below the line; stick (right hand) notes above the line

'x' note-heads show immediately-damped left-hand beats
~~~~

4. Music for *Qin*: Meihua san nong

6
♩ = c.121
Qin
125
130
135
140
7
♩ = c.116
145
150
155
160
165
170

175
180
8
♩ = c.123
185
190
195
200
205
9
♩ = c.125
210
215
220
225
230
235
rit.
240
etc.

Transcription Notes Barlines are inserted only for ease of reference, not to show metrical structure

↗ glissando (pitch slide) in direction indicated

⁀ notes slurred in a group resulting from a single pluck

○ harmonic

♩ note plucked simultaneously on two strings

5. Jiangnan *Sizhu* Ensemble Music: Huanle ge

The piece is performed three times – fast, medium and slow. This transcription concentrates on one instrument – the *dizi* (flute) – and shows the opening of each rendition, aligned for comparison.

♩ = c.38 (with gradual accel.)
1st rendition (slow)
[wood block]
♩ = c.78 (with gradual accel.)
2nd rendition (medium)
♩ = c.280 (with gradual accel.)
3rd rendition (fast)
tr
etc.

Transcription Notes Heterophonic parts for other instruments are omitted, as are the wood block beats

Chinese musicians would conceive rendition 3 in (the Chinese equivalent of) simple duple metre, i.e. with rhythmic values and metronome marking halved

6. *Chuanju* Opera: The Legend of White Snake

♩ = c.66
Chorus
Composite percussion rhythms
(solo)
(duo)
Wu yun man-tian [na - a] si [a - ao] hun
(clapper, gongs, drum & cymbal)
(clapper)
(solo)
(duo)
[ao] huang [a], Ji-dian gui - lai yu [a] duan
(gongs)
(clapper)
hun [a - - - - - a];
(gong & cymbal)
(gongs)
Solo singer
Lo-[i] dian dian, yu nin
(drum)
(cymbal)
(gong) (clapper)
nin, Neng yu zei lo [en] si da-[ao] yi-jin, Xin nan go,
(clapper)

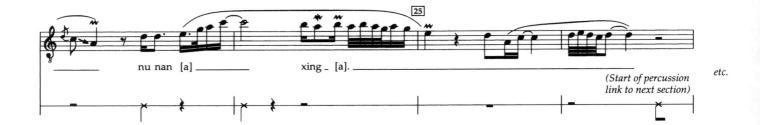

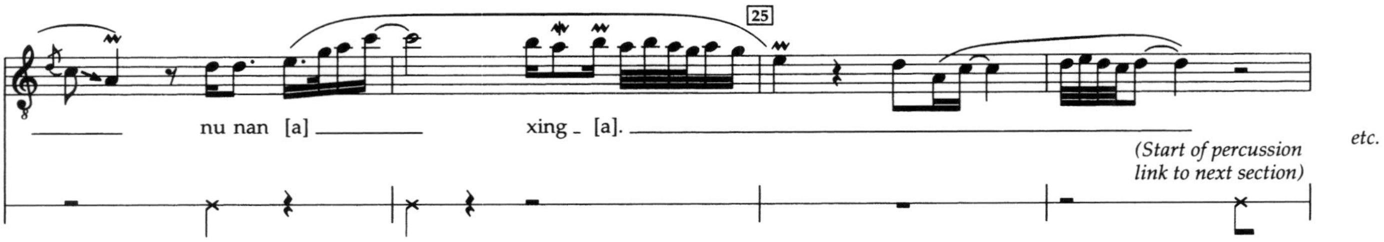
25
nu nan [a]
xing – [a].
(Start of percussion link to next section)
etc.

Transcription Notes

The upper stave compresses the vocal parts, beginning with the two female singers (the chorus) who sing both separately and together, and then showing the young male-role solo melody

the lower stave compresses percussion parts, including clapper, large and small gongs, cymbals and drum

↗ glissando (pitch slide) in direction indicated

[a] vocables, syllables of text without grammatical meaning

Transcribed one semitone above the recorded pitch

China: Tibet

7. Tibetan Ritual Music

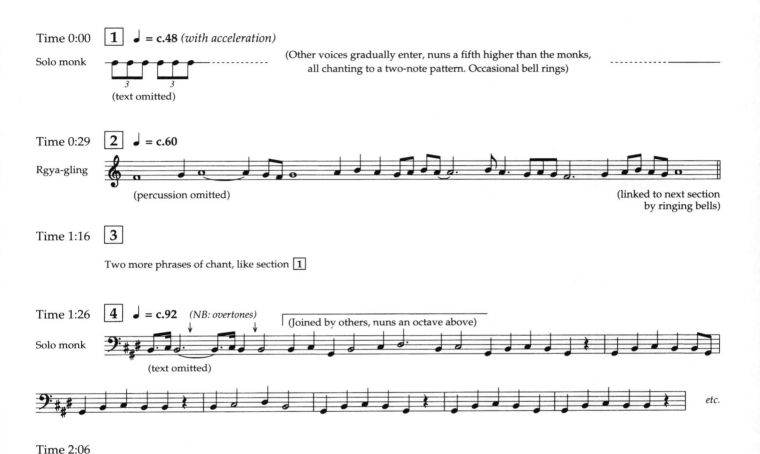

Time 0:00 **1** ♩ = c.48 *(with acceleration)*

Solo monk

(text omitted)

(Other voices gradually enter, nuns a fifth higher than the monks, all chanting to a two-note pattern. Occasional bell rings)

Time 0:29 **2** ♩ = c.60

Rgya-gling

(percussion omitted)

(linked to next section by ringing bells)

Time 1:16 **3**

Two more phrases of chant, like section 1

Time 1:26 **4** ♩ = c.92 *(NB: overtones)*

(Joined by others, nuns an octave above)

Solo monk

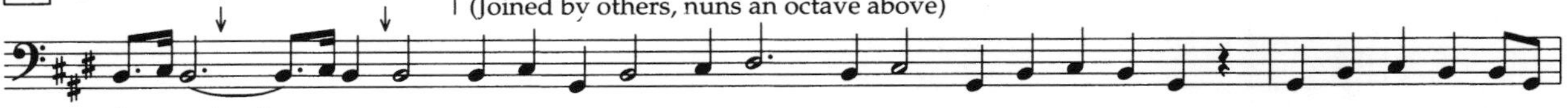

(text omitted)

etc.

Time 2:06

Transcription Notes

The transcription shows an excerpt from around one-third way through a three-hour ceremony. The remainder of the ceremony involves similar chanted, instrumental and sung passages to those illustrated here.

Percussion parts (bells, drums and cymbals) and all text are omitted

Melodic lines are outlines only, and are performed in heterophonic style

Barlines are used in section 4 to separate melodic patterns, and have no metrical sense

Mongolia

8. Diphonic Singing: Short song

1
♩ = c.83 (with slight acceleration)
Male voice
Normal voice (text omitted)
2
(♩ = c.91)
3
(♩ = c.94)
4
Overtone
ppp
cresc.
Fundamental
p
(hum – vowel sounds changing to produce overtones shown)
cresc.
5
ppp
p
6
tr

7
3

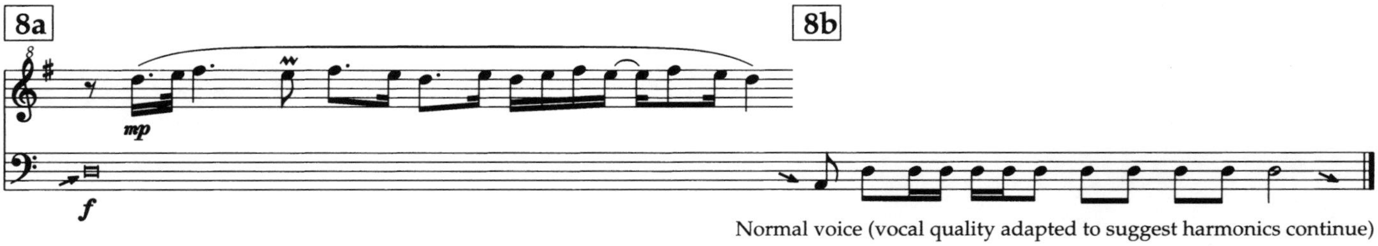
8a
8b
mp
f
Normal voice (vocal quality adapted to suggest harmonics continue)

Transcription Notes

Key signatures adapted to suit transcription

Text in phrases 1–3 and 8b omitted. No text sung in phrases 4–8a; instead, singer hums one pitch whilst altering his vocal cavity and tension (as if forming different vowel sounds) to produce overtones.

Rhythmic values approximate during phrases 4–8a

↗ vocal slide in direction shown

Vietnam

9. Music for *Dan Tranh*: Khong Minh toa lau

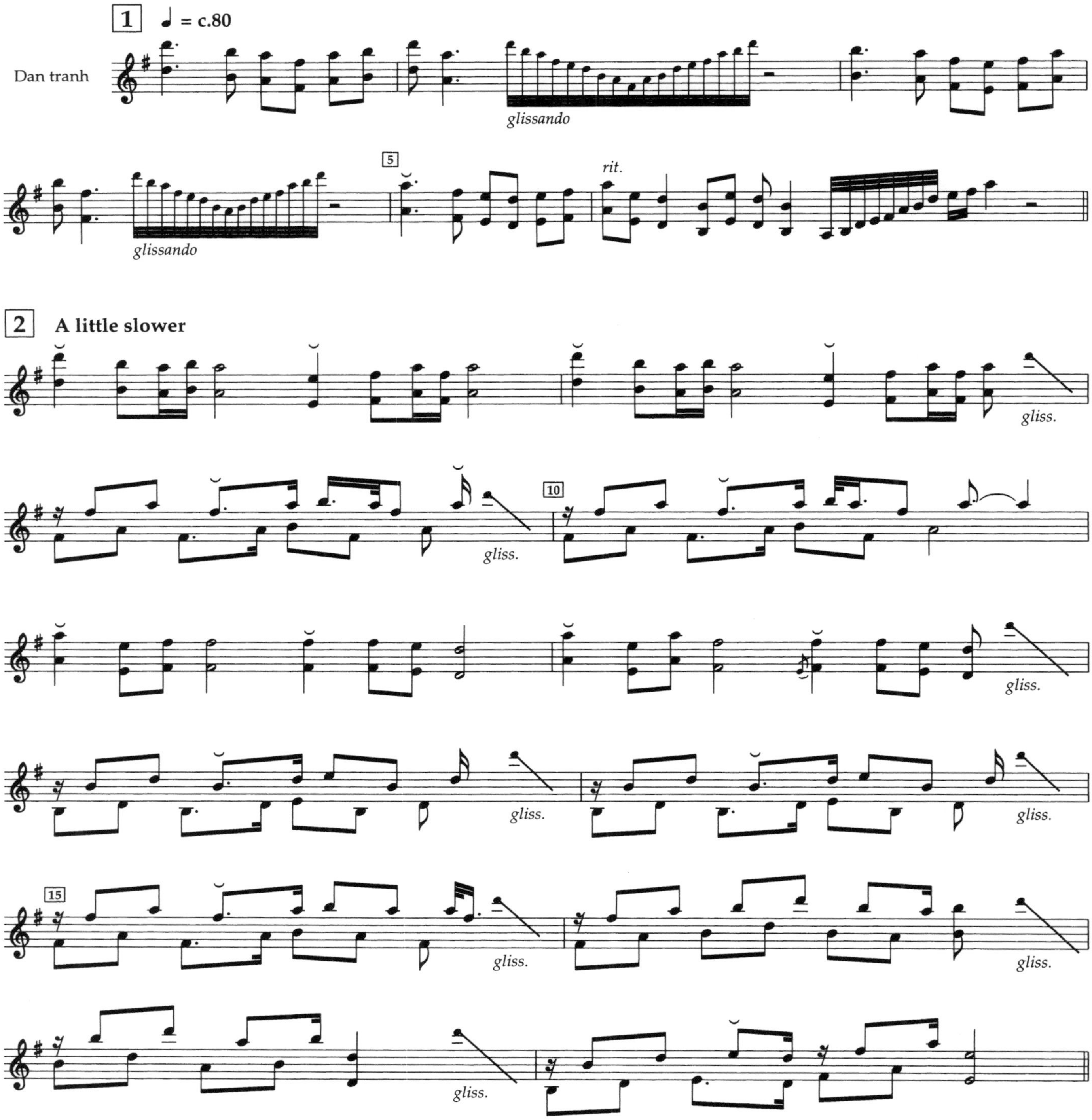

1
♩ = c.80
Dan tranh
glissando
glissando
5
rit.
2
A little slower
gliss.
10
gliss.
gliss.
gliss.
gliss.
15
gliss.
gliss.
gliss.

3 **A little faster**

20
25
rit.
30
gliss.
etc.

Transcription Notes

Pitches are not exactly equivalent to those of equal temperament

Barlines have been inserted only for ease of reference

Some octaves are performed slightly displaced, the lower pitch fractionally preceding the higher

gliss.

glissando, or strum across the strings, generally from top d'' down to a, lasting one quaver in duration

◡ note decorated by the player pushing on the string with the left fingers. Note the resulting 'pulsation' effect

10. Work Song: Ho hui

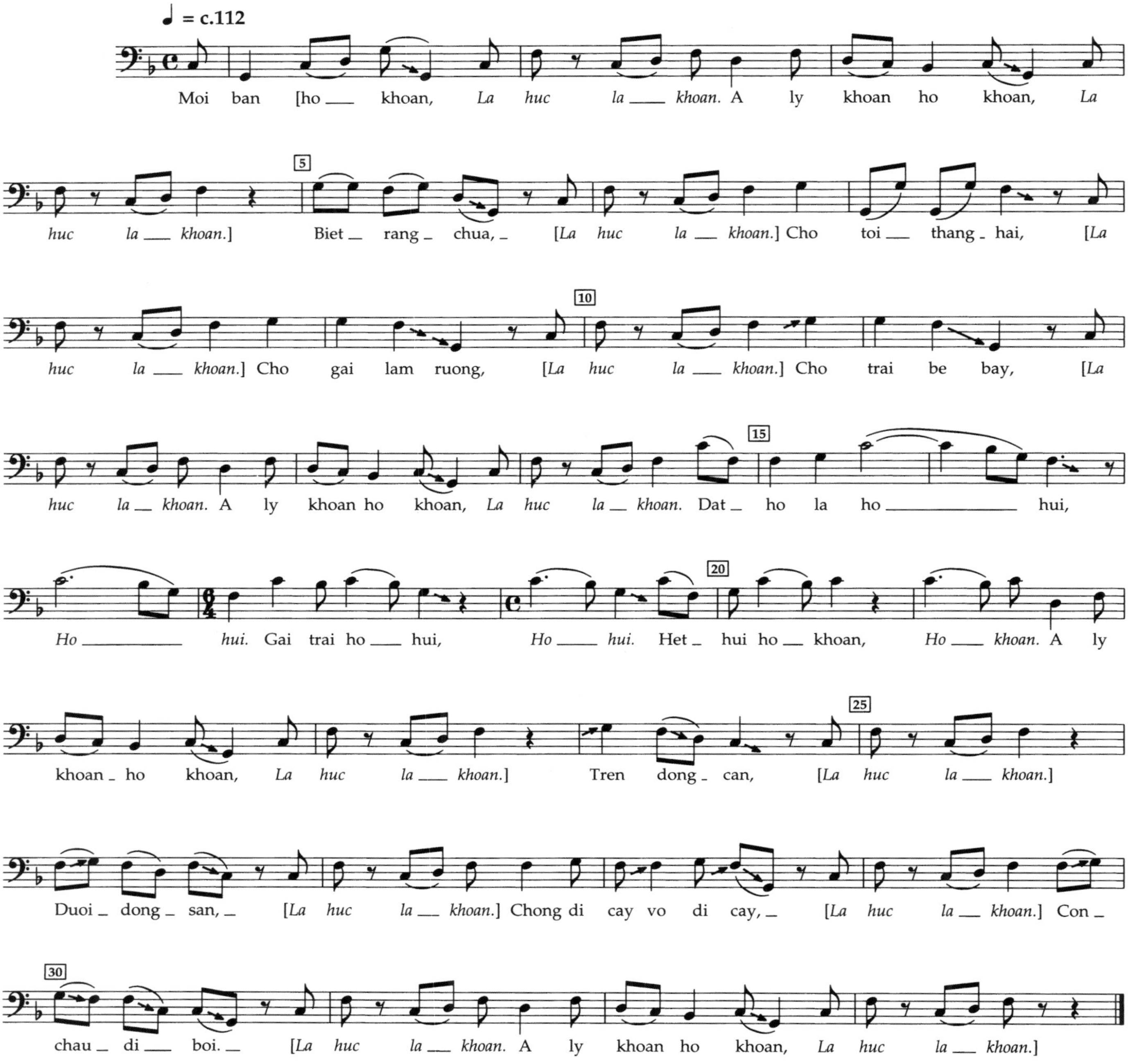
♩ = c.112
Moi ban [ho khoan, La huc la khoan. A ly khoan ho khoan, La
huc la khoan.] 5 Biet rang chua, [La huc la khoan.] Cho toi thang hai, [La
huc la khoan.] Cho gai lam ruong, 10 [La huc la khoan.] Cho trai be bay, [La
huc la khoan. A ly khoan ho khoan, La huc la khoan. 15 Dat ho la ho hui,
Ho hui. Gai trai ho hui, Ho hui. 20 Het hui ho khoan, Ho khoan. A ly
khoan ho khoan, La huc la khoan.] Tren dong can, 25 [La huc la khoan.]
Duoi dong san, [La huc la khoan.] Chong di cay vo di cay, [La huc la khoan.] Con
30 chau di boi. [La huc la khoan. A ly khoan ho khoan, La huc la khoan.]

Transcription Notes

The solo lines are printed in normal text, the chorus responses in italics (diacritical marks omitted)

Vocables are printed within square brackets

The chorus phrases are sung by two voices, one male and one female; the female voice an octave higher than notated

↗ glissando in direction indicated

Laos

11. Music for *Khāēn*: Nam phat khay

= c.88
drone
Khāēn
melody
etc.
5
10
15
20
25
30
35

40
45
50
etc.

Transcription Notes Reiterated B and F♯ drone maintained throughout (as in systems 1 and 2)

Some  rhythms are closer to 

Indonesia

12. Javanese Dance-Opera: Langen Mandra Wanara

1
Dalang
Sè - bet byar wahu les-ta-ri tin-da-ka-ri Ra - dyan Les-ma-na-wi-dag-da
lan Nar-pa - ti Su-gri - wa ing-kang ba-dé ka-dé-ré-ka-kan pa-ra ré-wan - da
so-wani-pun da-tèng Ne-ga - ri Ma - li - a - wan yèn si-na-wan sa-king man-dra - wa
bi - na-rung Sri Has - ca - ry - a swa - ra - ning pra - dang - - ga.

2 Gending ladrang Sri Hascarya

Introduction

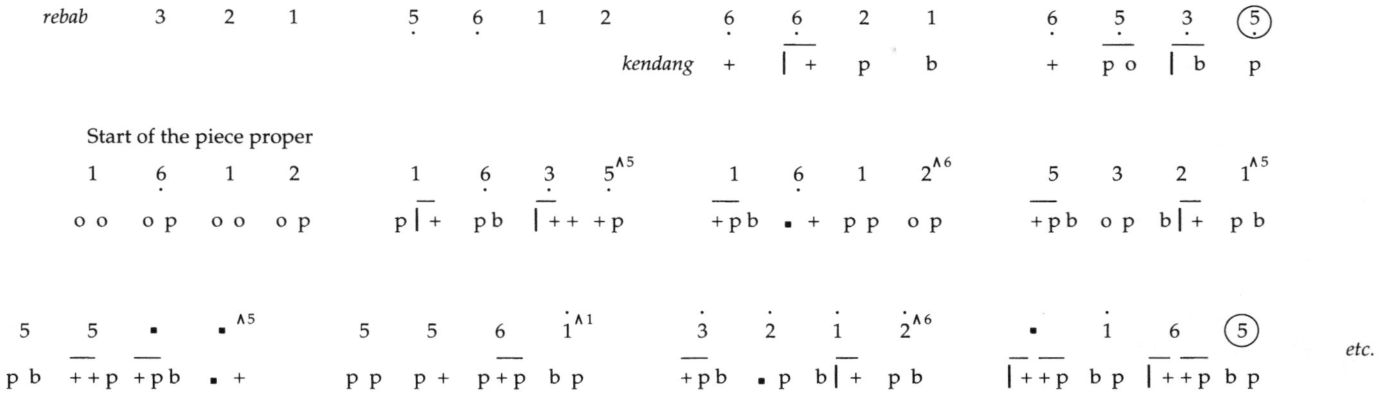
rebab
kendang
Start of the piece proper
etc.

Transcription Notes

Rhythmic and pitch values are only very approximate in section 1

The introduction to the gamelan piece has one drum beat to each main melodic note. From the start of the piece proper there are two beats to each main melody pitch

The tempo becomes regular from about the third four-note unit of the piece proper

Gong and melodic instrument notes (shown in Javanese cipher notation)

1, 2 etc. degrees of slendro tuning (main melody only shown – players expand this during performance to fully ornamented recorded version). Dots above/below notes indicate higher/lower octave.

- ▪ previous note sustained, repeated or a rest, depending upon the instrument
- ◯ stroke on the gong ageng
- ^5 stroke on another of the middle-sized or large gongs (pitch indicated)

Kendang (drum) strokes (shown in Javanese notation)

+	*tak*	LH gentle finger slap on centre of drumhead
o	*tong*	LH one or two fingers at edge
|	*ket*	RH one finger tap near centre
p	*dung*	RH one or more fingers bouncing stroke near centre
b	*bem*	RH all fingers bouncing stroke near edge
—		two strokes within this (metrical) beat
▪		rest

13. Balinese Music for *Gamelan Gong Gede*: Tabuh Pisan

♪ = c.176
Kendang
1
♩ = c.88
Gamelan (melodic outline)
(kendang continues)
gradual acceleration
5
10
15
20
25
rit.
30
35
2
♩ = c.116
(solo)
40
45
(+ kendang and lower gong)
(+ other instruments)
50
55
60
etc.

Transcription Notes

The intonation only broadly approximates to equal temperament

Transcribed one semitone above the recorded pitch

The transcription shows the main melodic outline only, and the kendang (drum) introduction

kendang symbols: resonant drum beat dry-sounding beat

14. Palawan Love Song: Kulilal at puguq

= c.144
Male voice
Pagang
Kusyapiq
[fade in on recording]
etc.
(kusyapiq continues to double the melody and provide a drone)
1
5
Njug du-wang ka-pu-hun,
Njug du-wang ka-pu-hun,
[Sam-pai-ke-ra.]
2
10
female voice (very soft indeed)
Ki-la ki-la ku na,
Ki-la ki-la ku na.
[Ki-la
Ki-la.]
[male voice speaks]
15
3
Tam-bang in ma-ba-tu,
Tam-bang in ma-ba-tu,
[In-an-bus-ka.]
etc.

Transcription Notes

The kusyapiq repeated bass drone and doubling of the melody continue throughout

[In-…] tentative transcription of vocables

Vocal phrases 1 and 2 are performed by a male singer, phrase 3 by a female voice

15. Music for *Aruding*: Lumalibang

= c.320
Aruding
5
10
15

Transcription Notes

The lower note (bass clef A) is the fundamental; treble clef notes show overtones favoured by alterations of the vocal cavity, tension and tongue position

Some  pairs are closer to  in rhythm

16. *Rihe* Panpipe Ensemble: Kikira

♩ = c.76
Melody
Drone
etc.
(overlapping continues)
Composite melody
(drone continues throughout)
5
10
1. 2.
15
3.

Transcription Notes

The overlapping drone continues throughout

The interlocking melody (as transcribed at the start) continues throughout

The barlines (once the tune settles into three-beat patterns) are for ease of reference only

Both repeats are varied in length as well as in melodic detail

* whistle – initially a high, falling sound, later the approximate pitches are shown

17. *Rope* Female Chorus: Ratsi Rope

♩ = c.38
Voice 1
[vowel sounds]
Voice 2
[vowel sounds]
Chorus
voices enter gradually, and periodically pause to breathe
1. 2. 3. 4.
5.

Transcription Notes

The text consists of vowel sounds (not transcribed). Slurs indicate patterns performed without rearticulation

Repeats varied

There is a slight pitch-drop during the performance

↗ pitch slide in direction indicated

Some ♫ pairs are closer to (3) ♪ ♩ in rhythm

Australia

18. Arnhem Land Aboriginal Music: Birruck

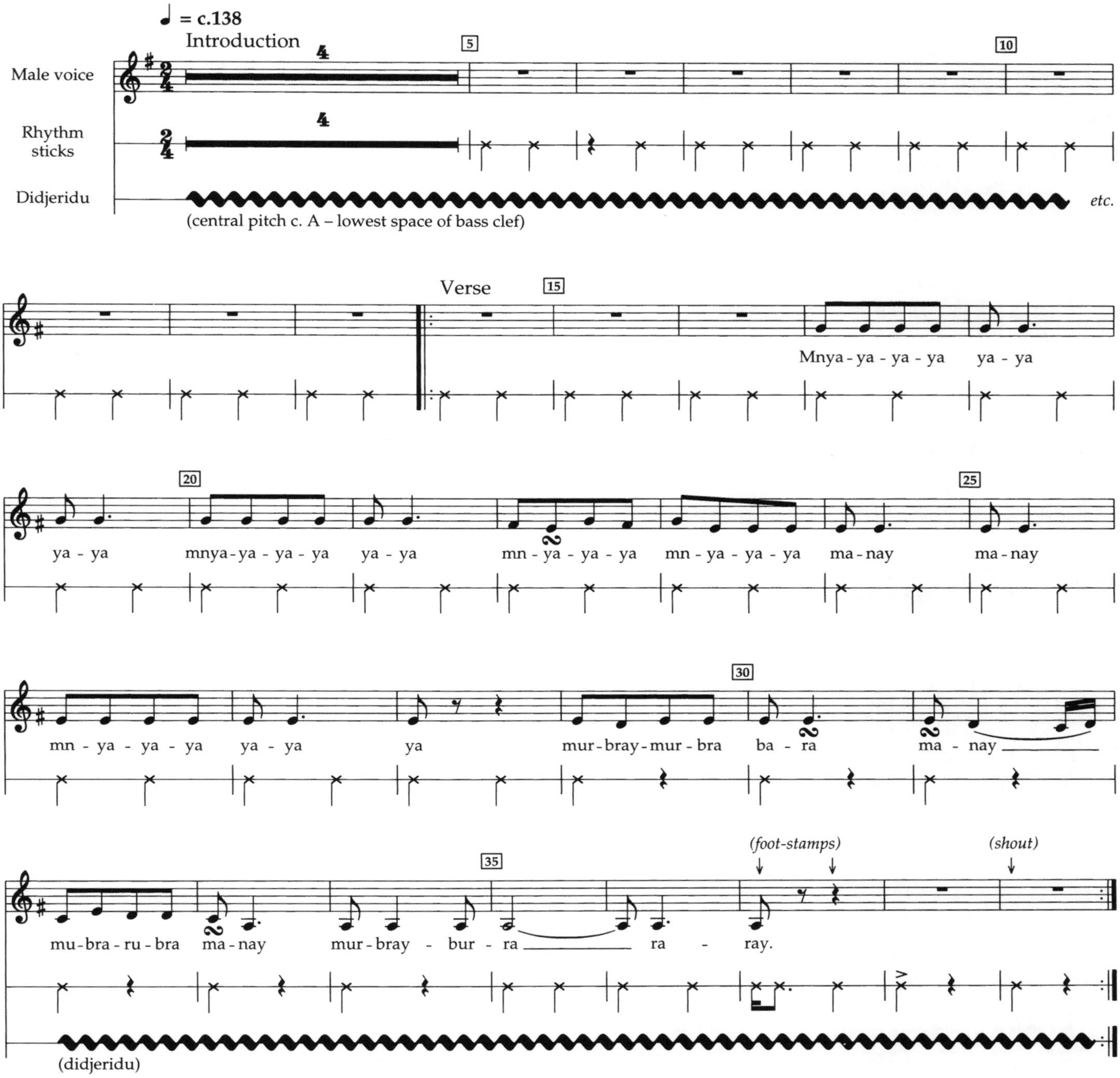
♩ = c.138
Introduction
Male voice
Rhythm sticks
Didjeridu
etc.
(central pitch c. A – lowest space of bass clef)
Verse
Mnya - ya - ya - ya ya - ya
ya - ya mnya-ya - ya - ya ya - ya mn - ya - ya - ya mn - ya - ya - ya ma - nay ma - nay
mn - ya - ya - ya ya - ya ya mur - bray - mur - bra ba - ra ma - nay
mu - bra - ru - bra ma - nay mur - bray - bur - ra ra - ray.
(foot-stamps)
(shout)
(didjeridu)

Transcription Notes

Barlines are used for convenience alone

Transcribed approximately one semitone above the recorded pitch

The verse section is performed four times, with minor alterations each time

The didjeridu plays throughout, stopping only at the very end

∾ vocal ornament or inflection

India

19. Music for *Vīnā*: Varnam

1
= c.92 (very free)
Vīnā
melody strings
rhythm strings
3
(from top to bottom)
(sim.)
(occasional strums on rhythm strings continue)
vibrato
vibrato

2
= c.108
Vīnā
Mrdangam
(strums on rhythm strings omitted)
5
10
15
etc.

Transcription Notes The rhythm strings are periodically reiterated throughout

Drum symbols:

 high-pitched, stopped note (approximate pitch E)

 high-pitched, unstopped note

 low-pitched note or notes with upward pitch alteration

20. Music for *Nāgasvaram*: Dudukulu Gaula

1
♩ = c.57
Nāgasvaram 1
Nāgasvaram 2 & 3
Sruti box
Tāvil
Tālam
4+2+2
4
(2 & 3)
(hand)
(stick)
tr
etc.
(2 & 3)

sruti box drone notes continue throughout

2
♩ = c.96
(2 & 3)
(2 & 3 stagger breathing)

etc.

Transcription Notes

The drone notes (sruti box) are maintained throughout

∿ melodic ornamentation (not transcribed)

↗ pitch slide in direction indicated

Drum symbols:

upper line: hand strike on higher-pitched drum face

lower line: stick strike on lower-pitched drum face

21. Music for *Pakhāvaj*: Ganesh Paran

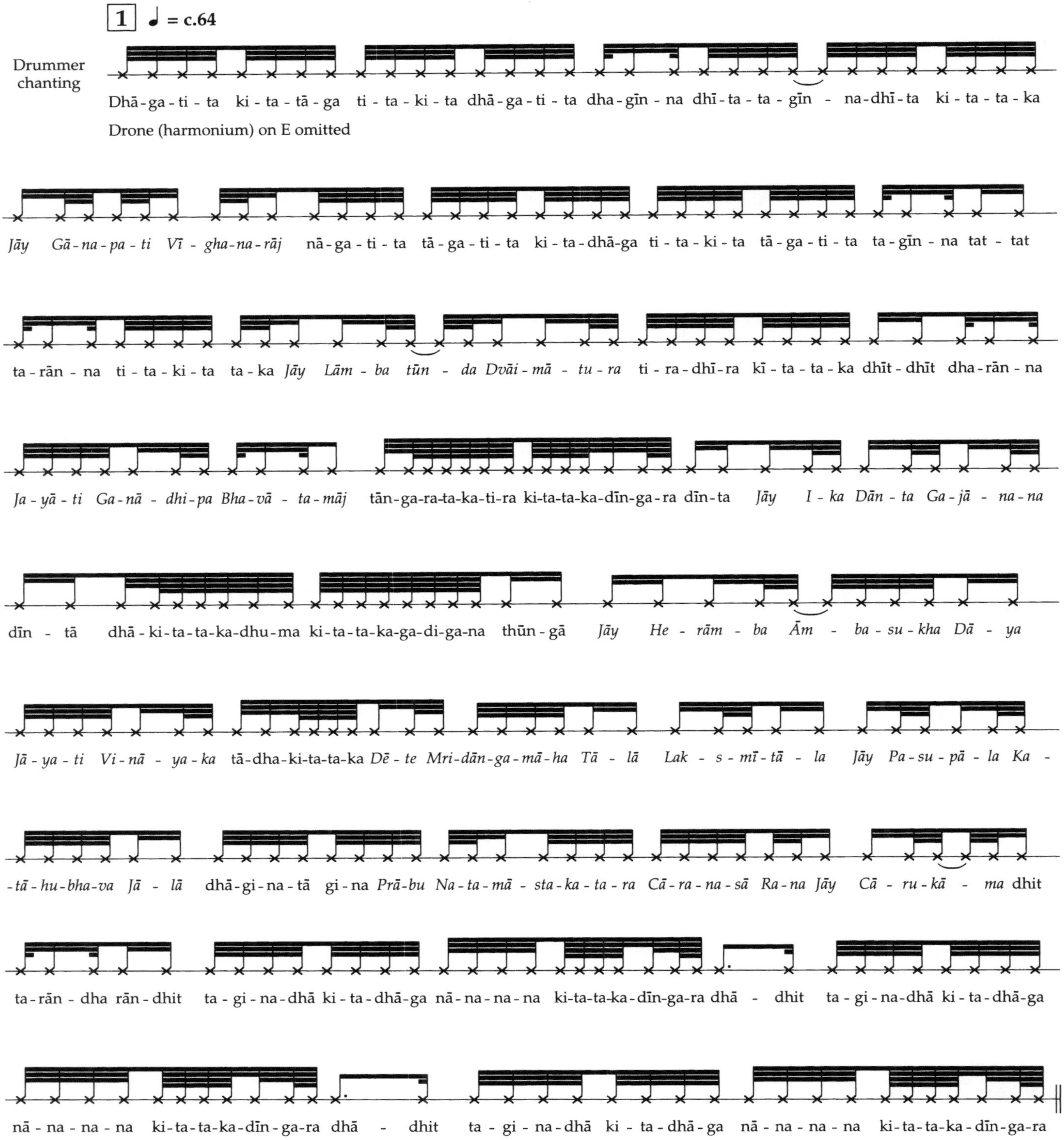
1 ♩ = c.64
Drummer chanting
Dhā-ga-ti-ta ki-ta-tā-ga ti-ta-ki-ta dhā-ga-ti-ta dha-gīn-na dhī-ta-ta-gīn - na-dhī-ta ki-ta-ta-ka
Drone (harmonium) on E omitted
Jāy Gā-na-pa-ti Vī-gha-na-rāj nā-ga-ti-ta tā-ga-ti-ta ki-ta-dhā-ga ti-ta-ki-ta tā-ga-ti-ta ta-gīn-na tat-tat
ta-rān-na ti-ta-ki-ta ta-ka Jāy Lām-ba tūn - da Dvāi-mā - tu-ra ti-ra-dhī-ra kī-ta-ta-ka dhīt-dhīt dha-rān-na
Ja-yā-ti Ga-nā - dhi-pa Bha-vā - ta-māj tān-ga-ra-ta-ka-ti-ra ki-ta-ta-ka-dīn-ga-ra dīn-ta Jāy I-ka Dān-ta Ga-jā - na-na
dīn - tā dhā-ki-ta-ta-ka-dhu-ma ki-ta-ta-ka-ga-di-ga-na thūn-gā Jāy He-rām-ba Ām - ba-su-kha Dā - ya
Jā-ya-ti Vi-nā - ya-ka tā-dha-ki-ta-ta-ka Dē-te Mri-dān-ga-mā-ha Tā - lā Lak-s-mī-tā - la Jāy Pa-su-pā - la Ka -
-tā-hu-bha-va Jā - lā dhā-gi-na-tā gi-na Prā-bu Na-ta-mā - sta-ka-ta-ra Cā-ra-na-sā Ra-na Jāy Cā - ru-kā - ma dhit
ta-rān-dha rān-dhit ta-gi-na-dhā ki-ta-dhā-ga nā-na-na-na ki-ta-ta-ka-dīn-ga-ra dhā - dhit ta-gi-na-dhā ki-ta-dhā-ga
nā-na-na-na ki-ta-ta-ka-dīn-ga-ra dhā - dhit ta-gi-na-dhā ki-ta-dhā-ga nā-na-na-na ki-ta-ta-ka-dīn-ga-ra

2

Repeat of section 1, now played on pakhāvaj

3 **gradual increase in tempo**

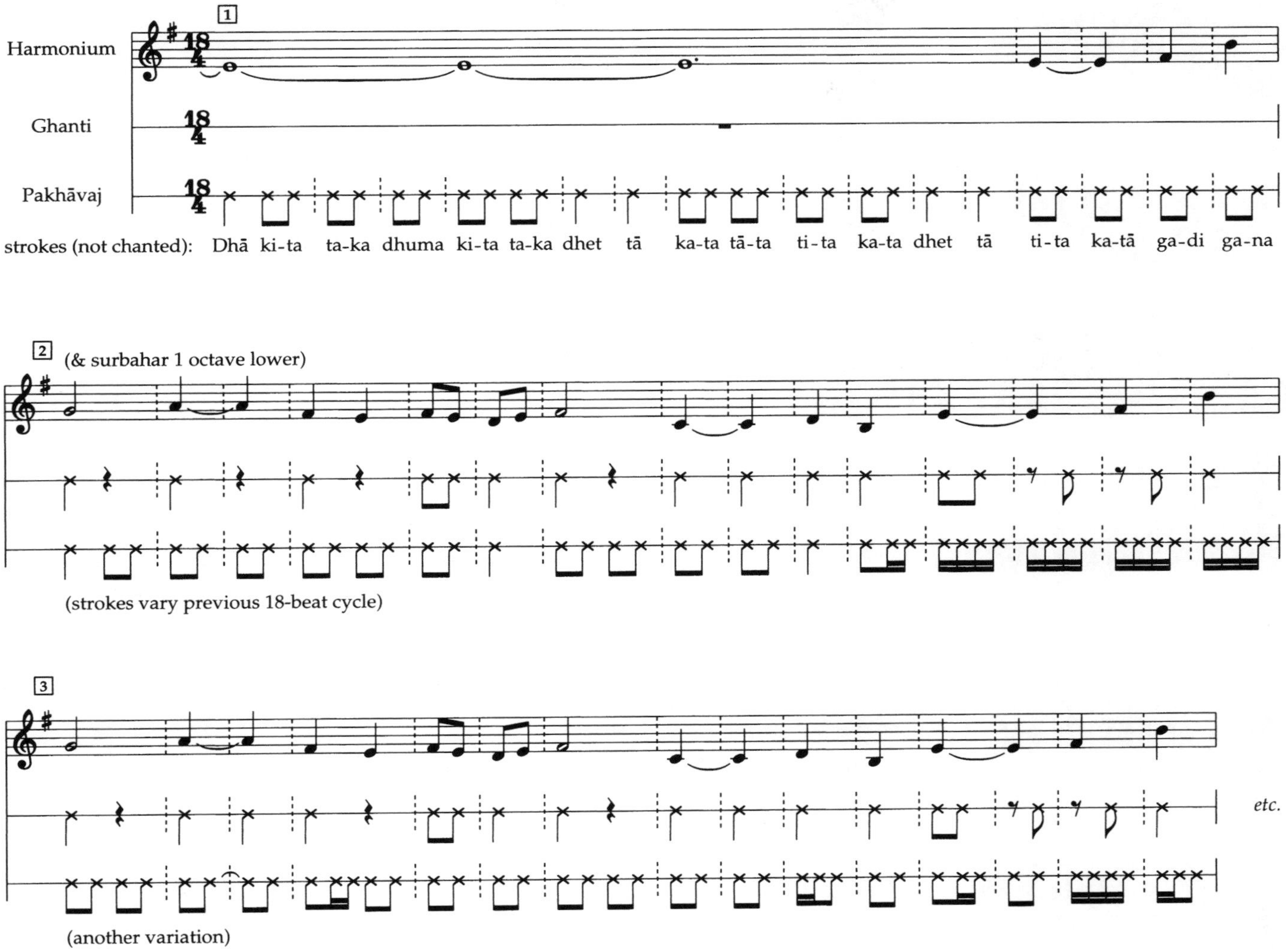
1
Harmonium
Ghanti
Pakhāvaj
strokes (not chanted): Dhā ki-ta ta-ka dhuma ki-ta ta-ka dhet tā ka-ta tā-ta ti-ta ka-ta dhet tā ti-ta ka-tā ga-di ga-na
2
(& surbahar 1 octave lower)
(strokes vary previous 18-beat cycle)
3
etc.
(another variation)

Transcription Notes

Transcribed slightly lower than the recorded pitch

The syllables printed in italics in section 1 are the actual text of an opening dedication; other syllables represent drum strokes

Examples of drum strokes:

dhā simultaneous LH undamped stroke partly on dough and RH slap with edge of hand on upper part of face slightly damped

kita RH two-stroke pattern using thumb, second and third fingers on centre, damped

na tap with RH finger on edge, undamped

Iran

22. Art Music for Ensemble: Tasnif Djan-e Djahan

Composite melodic outline
Composite percussion
♩ = c.98
5
13
(flute and strings)
p cresc.
f
percussion ostinato continues throughout
10
18
1.
20
25
(lower strings – shown only when melodic parts rest)
30
34
40
44
46
50
p
55
(melodic instruments continue)
melodic instruments
60
etc.
Voice (text omitted)
f
voice rests

Transcription Notes

The upper stave shows a composite of melodies played variously or separately by ney, santur, ud, tār and kamānche. Details of rhythm and ornamentation differ from one instrument to another

The lower stave shows a rhythmic ostinato performed on daf and zarb (and later doubled on lower strings). This is maintained throughout

𝄳 quartertone flat

Turkey

23. *Taksim* for *Ney*: Taksim Hüseyni

♩ = c.72
Ney
Kudüm
(kudüm continues)
to A
tr

65
70
75
80
85

Transcription Notes

The kudüm (drum) patterns similar to those in bars 1–8 are maintained throughout

The actual pitch of the ney is slightly lower than shown, and drops a little in the second half

𝄳 one comma flat (approximately an eighth of a tone)

↗ pitch slide in direction shown (rhythmic indications approximate during these passages)

Egypt

24. Quran Recitation: Surat Yusuf

♩ = c.78 (but very flexible)
1 A' ūdu bil - lāh - i min al - Shait - ān al - Raj - īm
2 bis - mil - lāh - i al - Rah - mān al - Rah - īm
3 Al - if La - m Ra'
4 til - ka Āy - ā - tu al - Kit - āb al - Mub - īn,
5 In - nā an - zal - nāh - u Qur - 'ān - an 'Ar - ab - īy - an la 'al - a - kum ta 'qil - ūn.
6 Nah - n - u na - qis - su 'Al - aik - a ah - san al - Qis - sas - i bim - ā 'au - hay - nā
il - aik - a hād - ā al - Qur - 'ān
7 bim - ā 'au - hay - nā il - aik - a hād - ā al -
- Qur - 'ān - a wa - in kun - ta min qhā - fil - īn il - ai min al - qhā - fi - līn.
etc.

Transcription Notes

The tempo is flexibly treated

Each number shows the beginning of a new phrase

↓ pitches marked with a downward arrow are slightly flatter than their equal-tempered equivalents

The D♮s in phrase 4 are a little sharper than their equal-tempered equivalent

tr▼ trill to the note below

↗ slide

25. *Taqsīm* for *Arghūl*

♩ = c.120
Arghūl
drone
etc.
slower ♩ = c.85
a tempo
tr
etc. (dance follows)
(drone)

Transcription Notes

Key signatures are used for convenience only; exact intonation is not based on equal temperament

Pitches remain affected by accidentals until end of staff or until cancelled, whichever is the sooner

The drone pitch (B) is maintained throughout the piece

↗ glissando (pitch slide) in direction indicated

26. Music for Folk Ensemble: Yā Farawla

5
♩ = c.126
80
Darabukka
Duff
Rabāba and Suffāra
etc.
etc.
(drums continue)
85
90
sim.
tr
95
suffāra
rabāba
sim.
Voice
Suffāra
(text omitted)
(rabāba continues)

(two beats added in repeat)
100
(gradually joined by other voices)
sim.
(two beats added in repeat)
Leader
105
(two beats added in repeat)
Chorus
(part of chorus)
rabāba
(suffāra omitted)
leader
110
1.
Chorus and leader exchange
roles during the repeat
6
(performed 5 times: leader, chorus alternately)
etc.
(drums and melodic instruments continue)

Transcription Notes

Three rabāba and one suffāra parts have, in general, been compressed into a single melodic outline. Where the suffāra part is not individually indicated, it plays an octave above the rabāba line

The drum rhythms have been transcribed as unpitched notes. However, higher and lower pitched notes on the duff are distinguished by placement above or below the single-line stave

Details of ornamentation are only selectively transcribed

Text omitted

↗ glissando (pitch slide) in direction indicated

⊳ half-sharp, i.e. pitches affected by this symbol are played a quartertone sharp

Morocco

27. *Nawba* Music for Ensemble: Nawba hijāzī al-kabīr

1
♩ = c.60
Composite melodic outline
(varied repeat of earlier material)
2
♩ = c.84 (and gradually a little faster)
(percussion added)
5
17
10
22
25
30
(1st time)
(2nd time)
(Bars 28–34 repeated to complete introduction. First song follows.)

Transcription Notes

The main melodic outline is transcribed, with individual instrumental variations largely omitted

The tār (tambourine) part from section 2 – mainly semiquavers – is omitted

𝄳 quartertone flat

Algeria

28. Music for *Ghayta* and *Bendīr*: Dance from the Aurès Mountains

♩ = c.135
Ghayta
Bendīr
etc.
(bendīr rhythm continues throughout)

tr
75
80
85
90
(bendīr)

Transcription Notes The bendīr pattern transcribed in bars 1–6 is maintained until the final few seconds

The intonation of the ghayta part is not modelled on equal temperament

Vibrato is used on the ghayta throughout

Mali

29. Griot Song: Duga

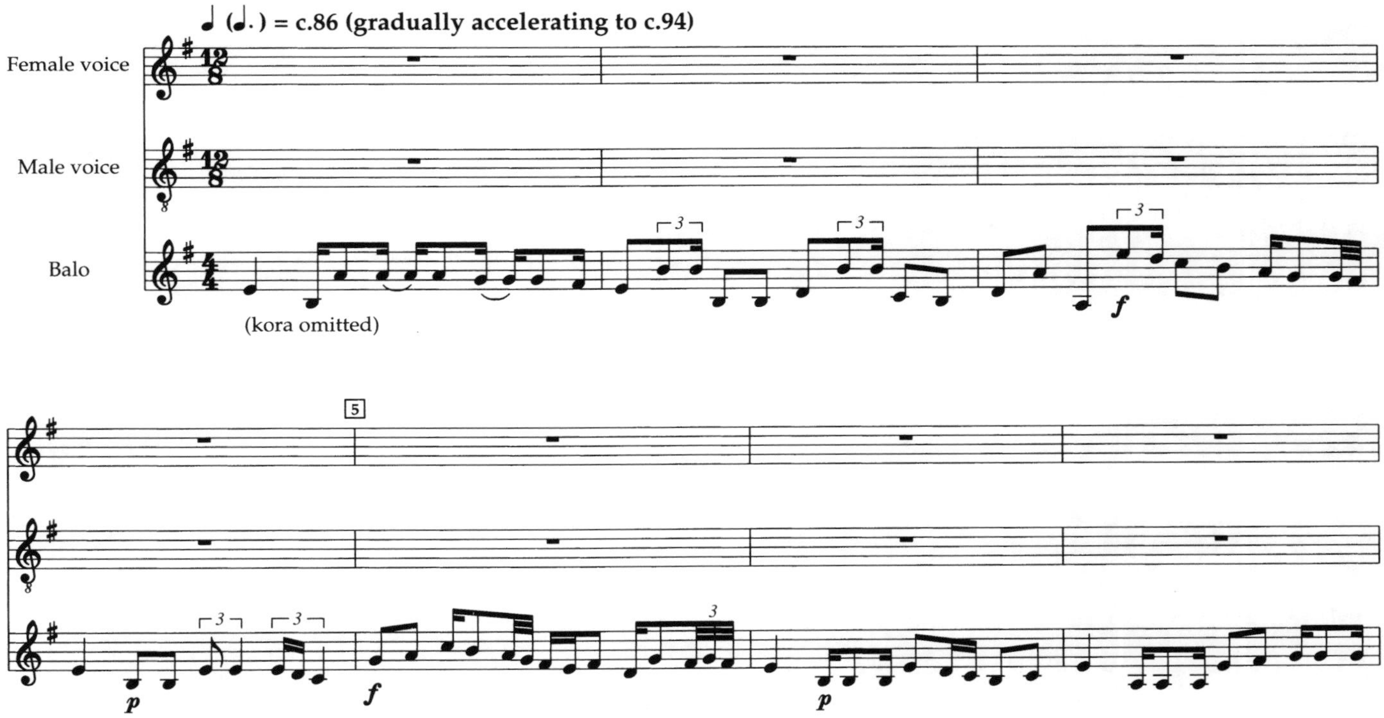
♩ (♩.) = c.86 (gradually accelerating to c.94)
Female voice
Male voice
Balo
(kora omitted)
3
5
f
p

10
(text omitted)
(unclear)
15
(text omitted)
20
25

30
f
3
35
40
45
3
etc.

Transcription Notes

Transcribed one semitone above the recorded pitch

The mostly heterophonic accompaniment part for kora (harp-lute) is omitted

Text omitted

↗ pitch slide in direction marked

Ethiopia

1. Song with masenqo

1
♩ = c.104
Masenqo
2
Male voice
(text omitted)
masenqo doubles voice
3
voice rests
4
5
6
7
8
9
10
11
12
13
14
etc.

Transcription Notes

Passages in [ ] are masenqo solos, passages outside brackets are vocal lines. At these points, the masenqo performs a decorated form of the vocal line

Each alternation of instrument and instrument-plus-voice is numbered for reference

Text omitted

∾ vocal ornamentation (not transcribed)

2. Chorus: Dama

♩ = c.124
Female voice
Solo voice
Da - ma eh _ da - ma, etc.
Chorus
A-hey _ da-ma dan-si, etc.
Vocables
Eh _ eh _ eh _
Hand-claps
5
etc. Eh eh
Chorus and hand-claps continue
Sporadic entries of vocables
Male voice only
10
Male voice enters
vocables gradually fall into following pattern:
etc.
(composite pattern – each note sustained by a different voice)
15
20
etc.

Transcription Note The transcription shows the main outline only

Central African Republic

3. Song with *Sanza*: Nàá-Ndongoé

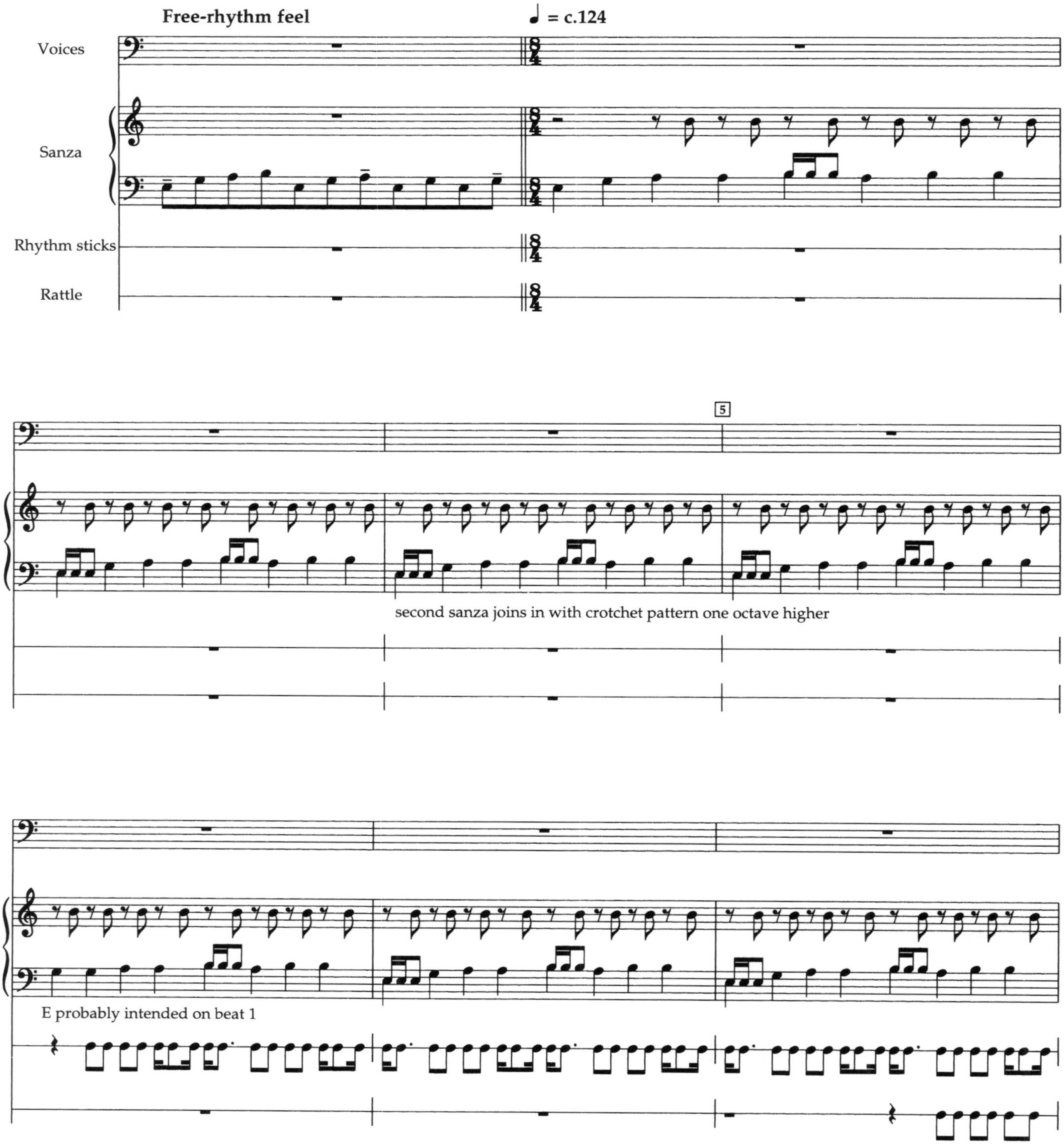
Free-rhythm feel
♩ = c.124
Voices
Sanza
Rhythm sticks
Rattle
5
second sanza joins in with crotchet pattern one octave higher
E probably intended on beat 1

10
1st voice
2nd voice
(humming)
(sings) text omitted
six times in total
etc.

Transcription Notes Intonation not quite equivalent to equal temperament

Song text and second sanza part omitted

Gabon

4. Yodelling exercise

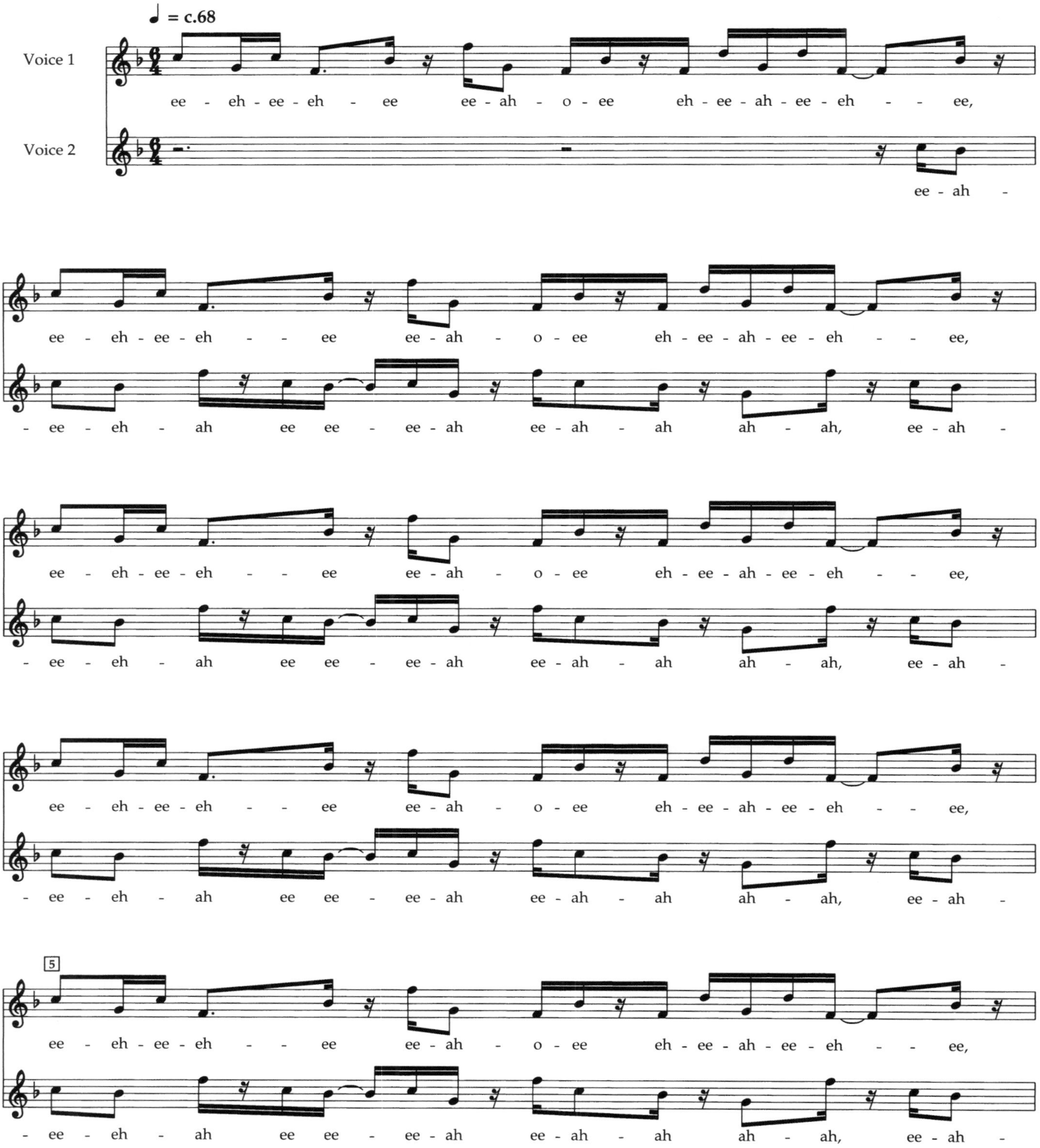
♩ = c.68
Voice 1
ee - eh - ee - eh - ee ee - ah - o - ee eh - ee - ah - ee - eh - - ee,
Voice 2
ee - ah -
ee - eh - ee - eh - - ee ee - ah - o - ee eh - ee - ah - ee - eh - - ee,
- ee - eh - ah ee ee - ee - ah ee - ah - ah ah - ah, ee - ah -
ee - eh - ee - eh - - ee ee - ah - o - ee eh - ee - ah - ee - eh - - ee,
- ee - eh - ah ee ee - ee - ah ee - ah - ah ah - ah, ee - ah -
ee - eh - ee - eh - - ee ee - ah - o - ee eh - ee - ah - ee - eh - - ee,
- ee - eh - ah ee ee - ee - ah ee - ah - ah ah - ah, ee - ah -
5
ee - eh - ee - eh - - ee ee - ah - o - ee eh - ee - ah - ee - eh - - ee,
- ee - eh - ah ee ee - ee - ah ee - ah - ah ah - ah, ee - ah -

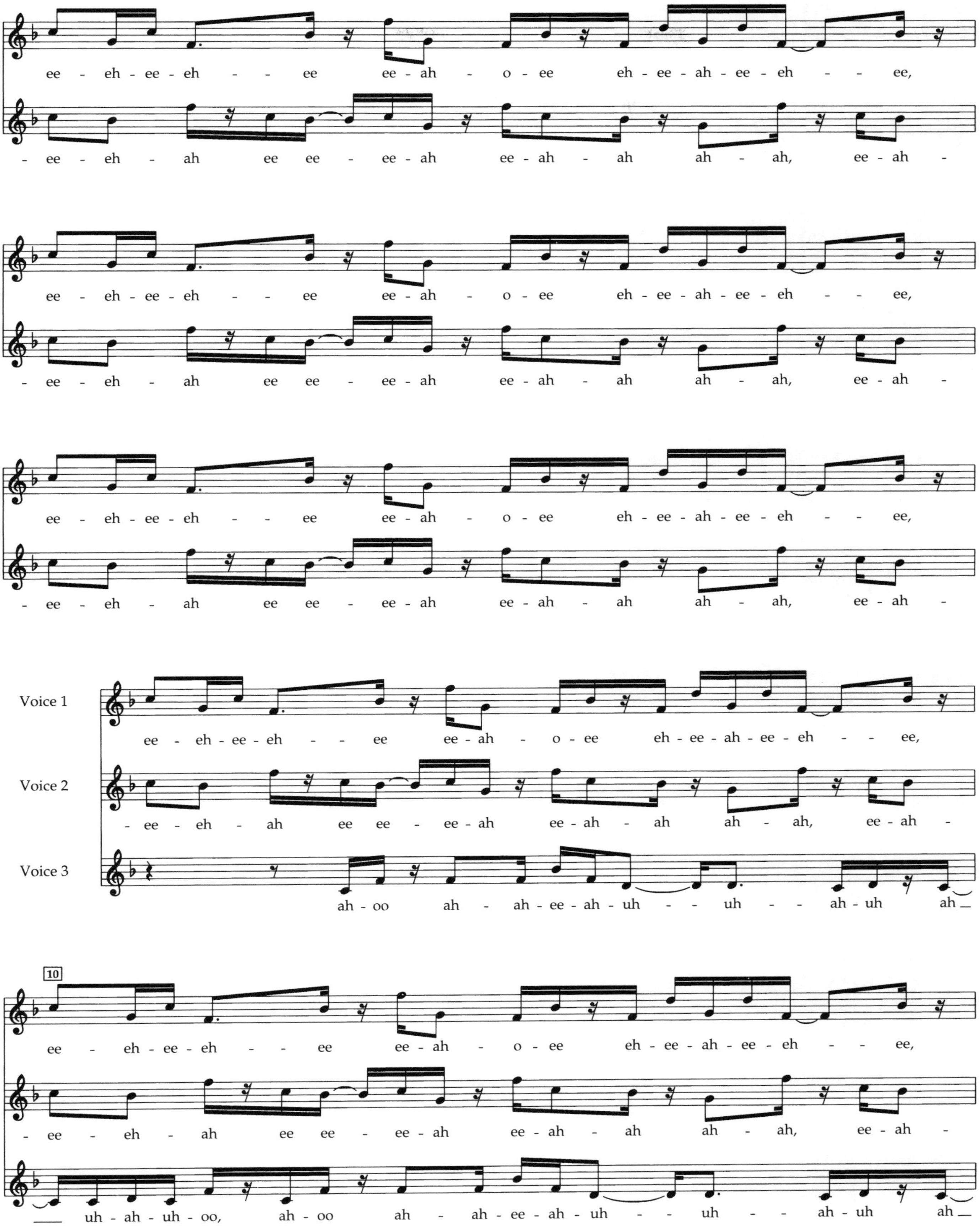
ee - eh - ee - eh - - ee ee - ah - o - ee eh - ee - ah - ee - eh - - ee,
- ee - eh - ah ee ee - ee - ah ee - ah - ah ah - ah, ee - ah -
ee - eh - ee - eh - - ee ee - ah - o - ee eh - ee - ah - ee - eh - - ee,
- ee - eh - ah ee ee - ee - ah ee - ah - ah ah - ah, ee - ah -
ee - eh - ee - eh - - ee ee - ah - o - ee eh - ee - ah - ee - eh - - ee,
- ee - eh - ah ee ee - ee - ah ee - ah - ah ah - ah, ee - ah -
Voice 1
ee - eh - ee - eh - - ee ee - ah - o - ee eh - ee - ah - ee - eh - - ee,
Voice 2
- ee - eh - ah ee ee - ee - ah ee - ah - ah ah - ah, ee - ah -
Voice 3
ah - oo ah - ah - ee - ah - uh - - uh - - ah - uh ah
10
ee - eh - ee - eh - - ee ee - ah - o - ee eh - ee - ah - ee - eh - - ee,
- ee - eh - ah ee ee - ee - ah ee - ah - ah ah - ah, ee - ah -
uh - ah - uh - oo, ah - oo ah - ah - ee - ah - uh - - uh - - ah - uh ah

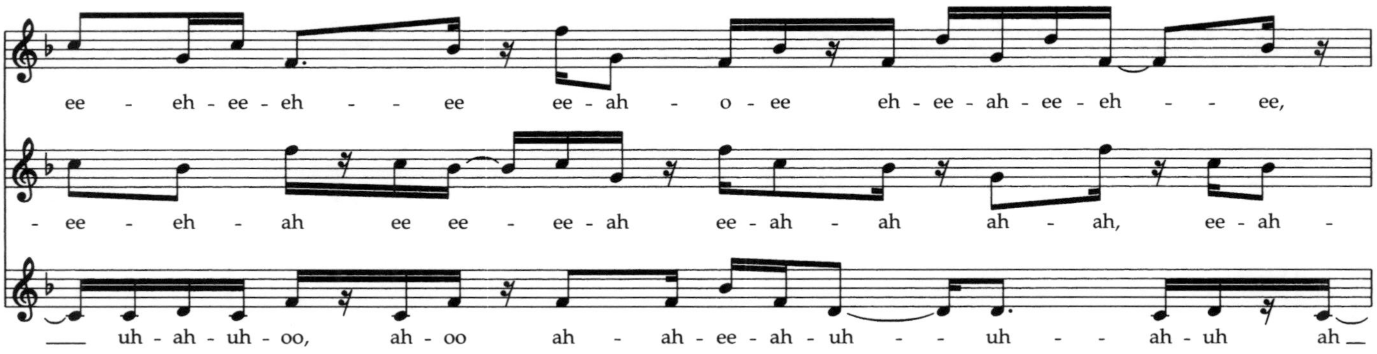
ee - eh - ee - eh - - ee ee - ah - o - ee eh - ee - ah - ee - eh - - ee,
- ee - eh - ah ee ee - ee - ah ee - ah - ah ah - ah, ee - ah -
uh - ah - uh - oo, ah - oo ah - ah - ee - ah - uh - - uh - - ah - uh ah

Performed 12 times, with occasional, minor variations

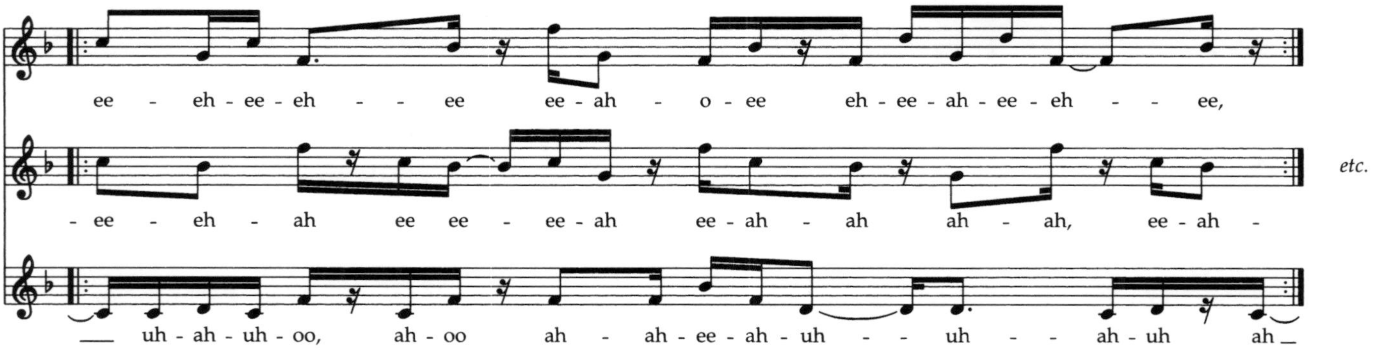
ee - eh - ee - eh - - ee ee - ah - o - ee eh - ee - ah - ee - eh - - ee,
- ee - eh - ah ee ee - ee - ah ee - ah - ah ah - ah, ee - ah -
etc.
uh - ah - uh - oo, ah - oo ah - ah - ee - ah - uh - - uh - - ah - uh ah

Transcription Notes F and B♭ are sung flatter than equal temperament; D somewhat sharper

The 'lyrics' are vowel sounds, not actual words

5. Whispered Song: Praise Song

♩ = c.118
Voice (rhythm only)
Inanga
An ma - ran da - ree ye,
an ma - ran da - ree ye,
an - du kum - bu ye - bi - ka bu,
5
an - du kum - bu ye - bi - ka bu,
a - to lay - mo - mee gen - de wa jo,
an - du kum - bu ye - mu tsu,
le - sim po - tsu nam - ba ra,
a - wan by - in ga - ne wan - kum - bu ye,
10
an - du kum - ba ye - lu - vin ka,
a - twa gen - dan ye - de - ta ken - za na,
a - ye twa - ba la - ro ye - ee ka,

na-mu ken-zee ne - fo sa,
na-mu kun - de men - say o - see a,
15
30 8
ki-la, ki-la, ki-la, ki-la, ki-la, ki-la, ki-la, ki-la, ki-la, ki-la, ki-la,
ki-la, ki-la, ki-la, ki-la, ki-la-say-vay en - zu gua min-ban gor,
20
ki-la, ki-la, ki-la, ki-la-sa na-sem gua-nam hu - za na we,

nin - ga nay - vu gee-da-wun ba - ing ga - wun ba - ing ga-nay-wun kum - bu ye,
kum - bu ye - en kum - bu ye - da kum - bu ye-mu-la mu - nai je,
nee-wai-ya te-le-tse le - tsi an - dan dyen - gun ban - day va - un go,
etc.

Transcription Notes

The voice and inanga parts are performed by the same musician

C♯ and D♯ are sharper than in equal temperament

The rhythms of the inanga part are sometimes approximate

Vocal pitches omitted (the voice typically follows the outline of the instrumental melody)

In phonetic transcription of the text, single vowel 'a' as 'car', single 'e' as in 'where', 'g' as in 'go'; other letters as in standard English pronunciation

Hyphenation of syllables follows the metre (except for the repetition of 'kila')

6. Music for Ingoma

1

Single drum strike
Four solo calls, each answered by group cheers
One final solo call. (Total duration 15 seconds)

2

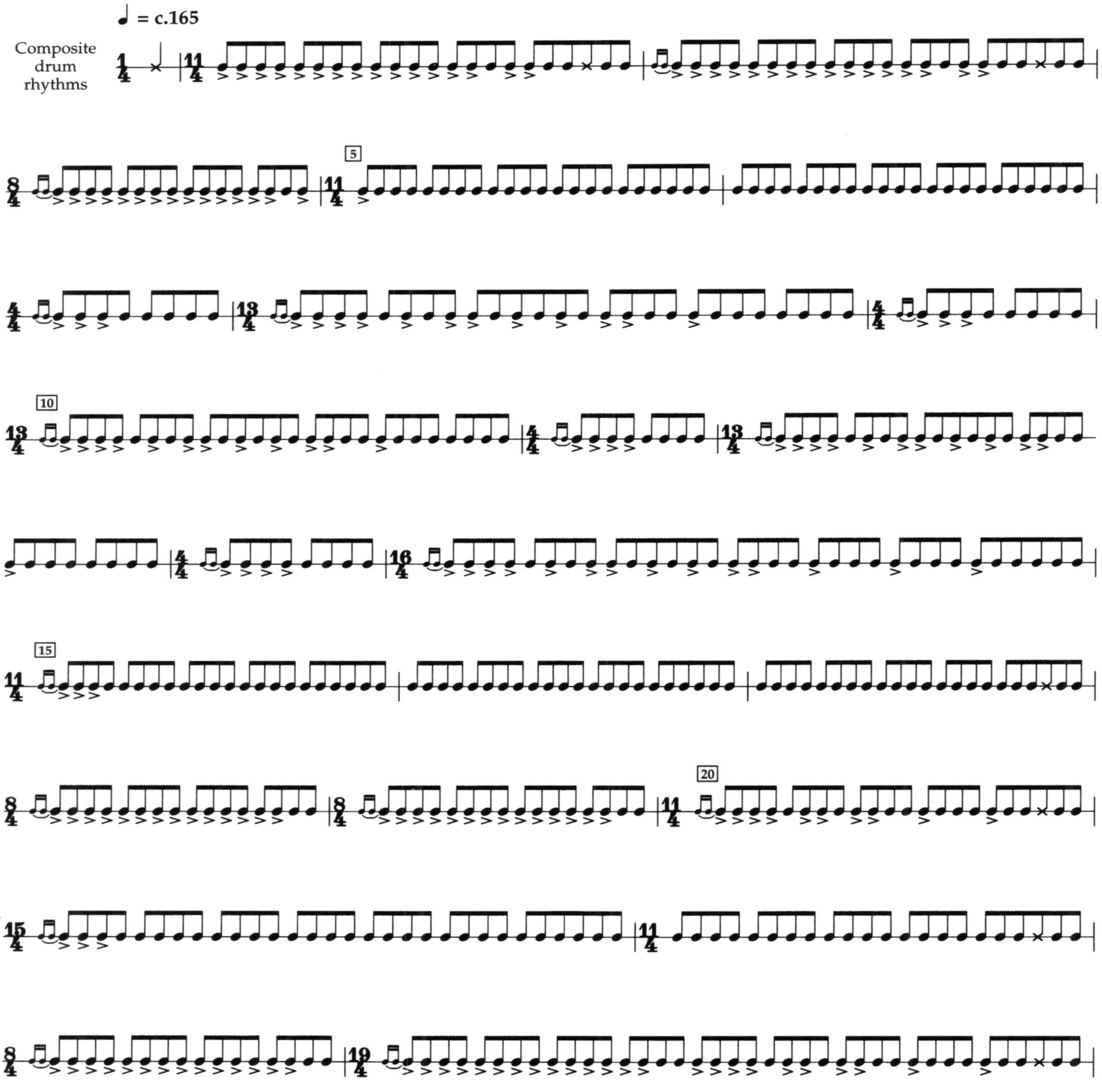

♩ = c.165
Composite drum rhythms
5
10
15
20

25
etc.

Transcription Notes

The transcription outlines the drum rhythms and accents. Metre and note-groupings are arranged to make repetition of rhythmic patterns more apparent

Solo calls and responding group cheers (for example, bar 5) are omitted

'x' note-heads represent drier-sounding strikes (stick on stick?)

7. Child's Song: Song with umuduri

♩ = c.124
Voice
(text omitted)
Umuduri
umuduri continues same pattern throughout
5
10
15
20
(sings a little flat during this phrase)
25
etc.

Transcription Notes

The umuduri ostinato continues throughout

The rhythm of the final two quavers of each phrase is sometimes closer to two dotted quavers (no rest before barlines)

↗ pitch slide in direction shown

8. Music for *Timbila*: Mabandla

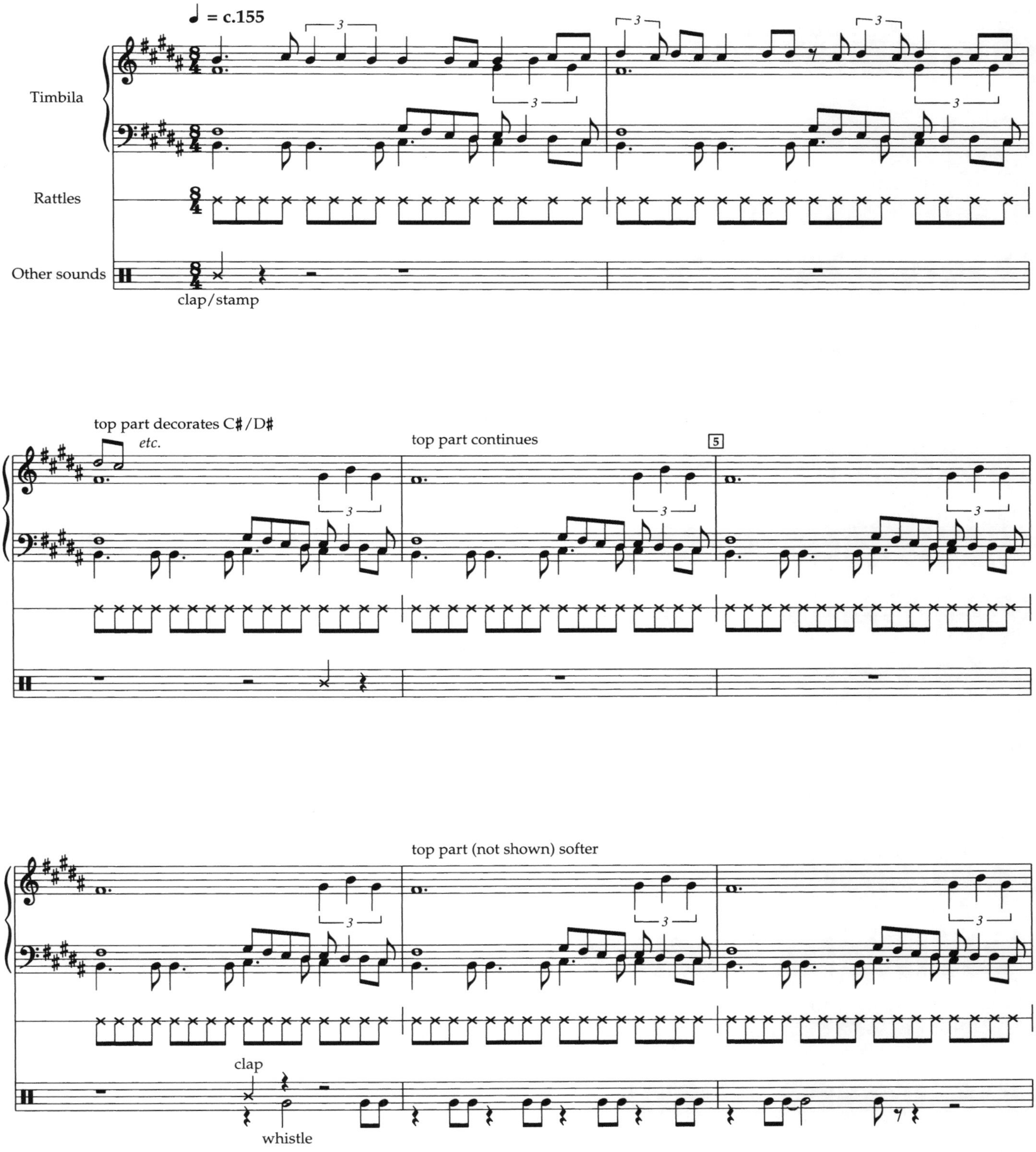
♩ = c.155
Timbila
Rattles
Other sounds
clap/stamp
top part decorates C♯/D♯
etc.
top part continues
5
top part (not shown) softer
clap
whistle

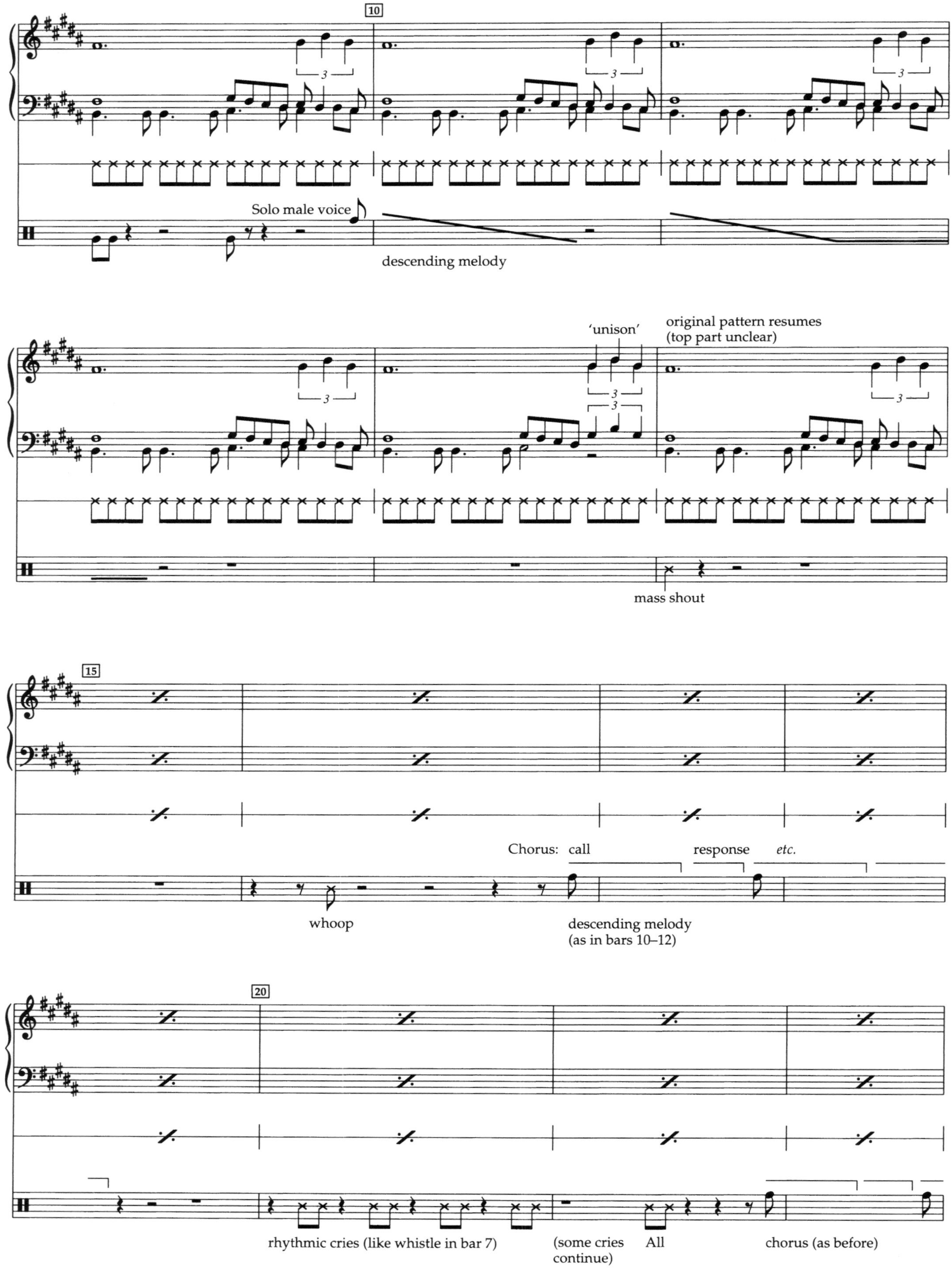
10
Solo male voice
descending melody
'unison'
original pattern resumes
(top part unclear)
mass shout
15
Chorus: call
response
etc.
whoop
descending melody
(as in bars 10–12)
20
rhythmic cries (like whistle in bar 7)
(some cries
continue)
All
chorus (as before)

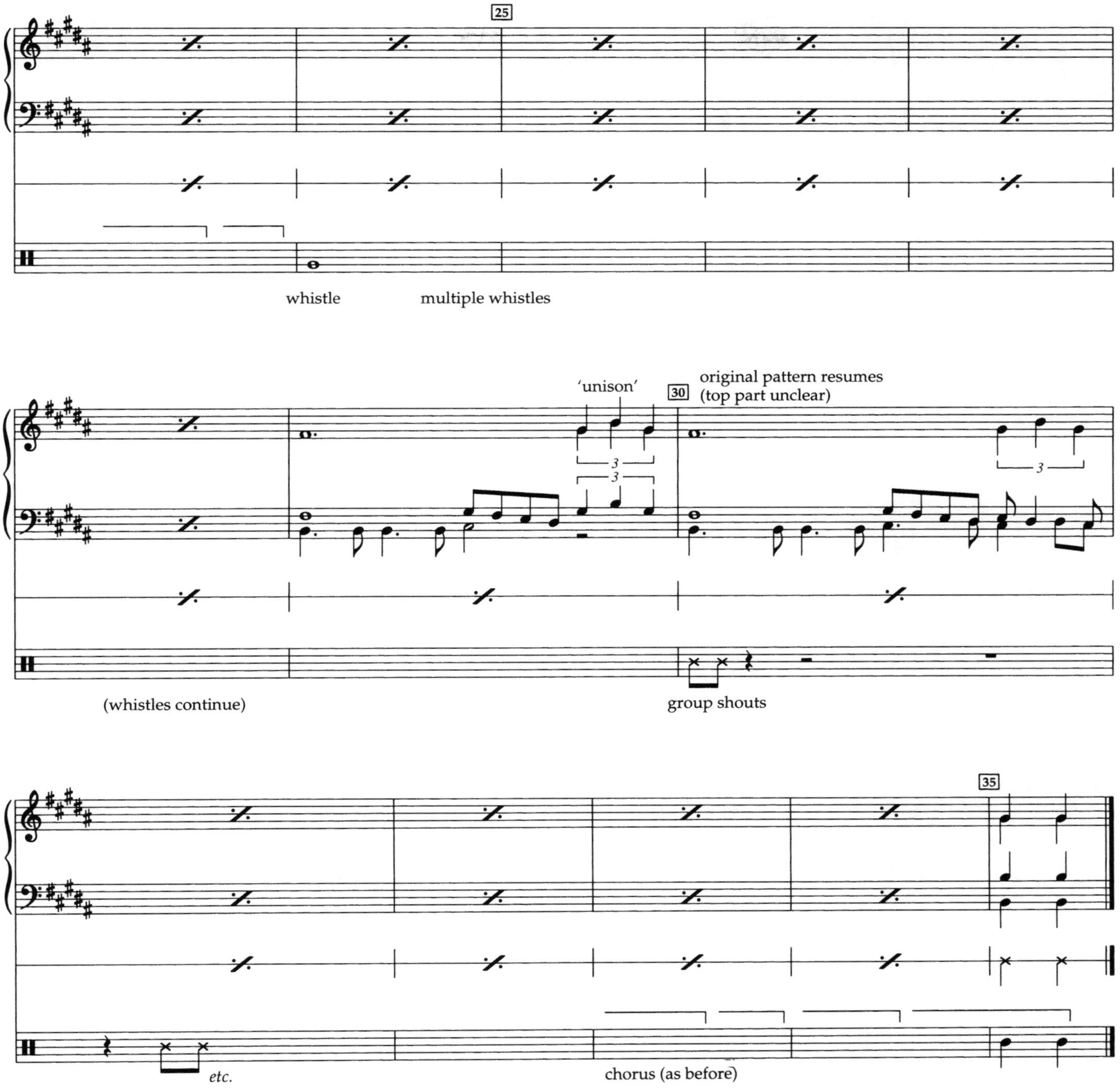
25
whistle
multiple whistles
'unison'
30
original pattern resumes
(top part unclear)
(whistles continue)
group shouts
35
etc.
chorus (as before)

Transcription Notes

The transcription shows an outline of the piece only, largely omitting complex upper and middle xylophone parts

Intonation follows equidistant heptatonic scale

Russia

9. Play Song

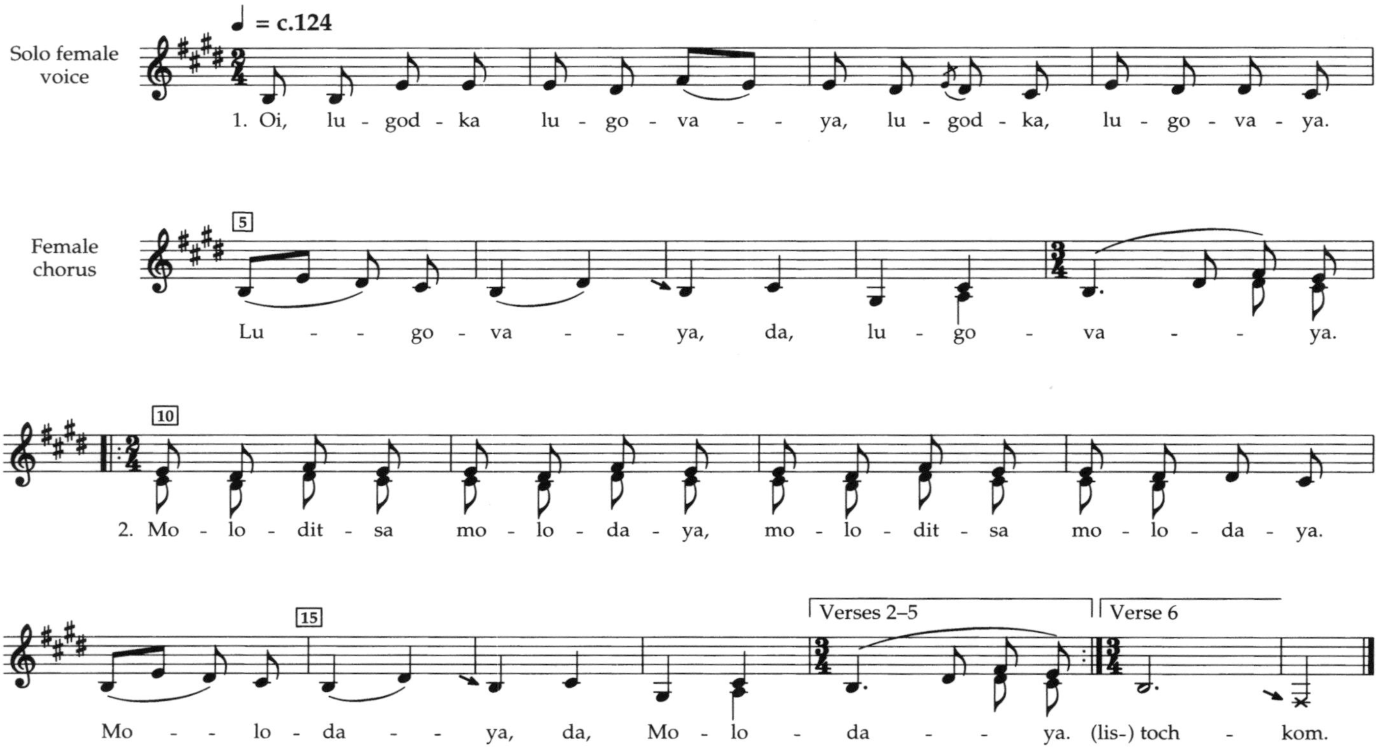

♩ = c.124
Solo female voice
1. Oi, lu - god - ka lu - go - va - - ya, lu - god - ka, lu - go - va - ya.
Female chorus
5
Lu - - go - va - - ya, da, lu - go - va - - ya.
10
2. Mo - lo - dit - sa mo - lo - da - ya, mo - lo - dit - sa mo - lo - da - ya.
15
Verses 2–5
Verse 6
Mo - - lo - da - - ya, da, Mo - lo - da - - ya. (lis-) toch - kom.

Transcription Notes

Texts given only for verses 1 and 2

↗ pitch slide in direction indicated

approximate pitch

Armenia

10. Hymn: Ognagan Induneli Egher

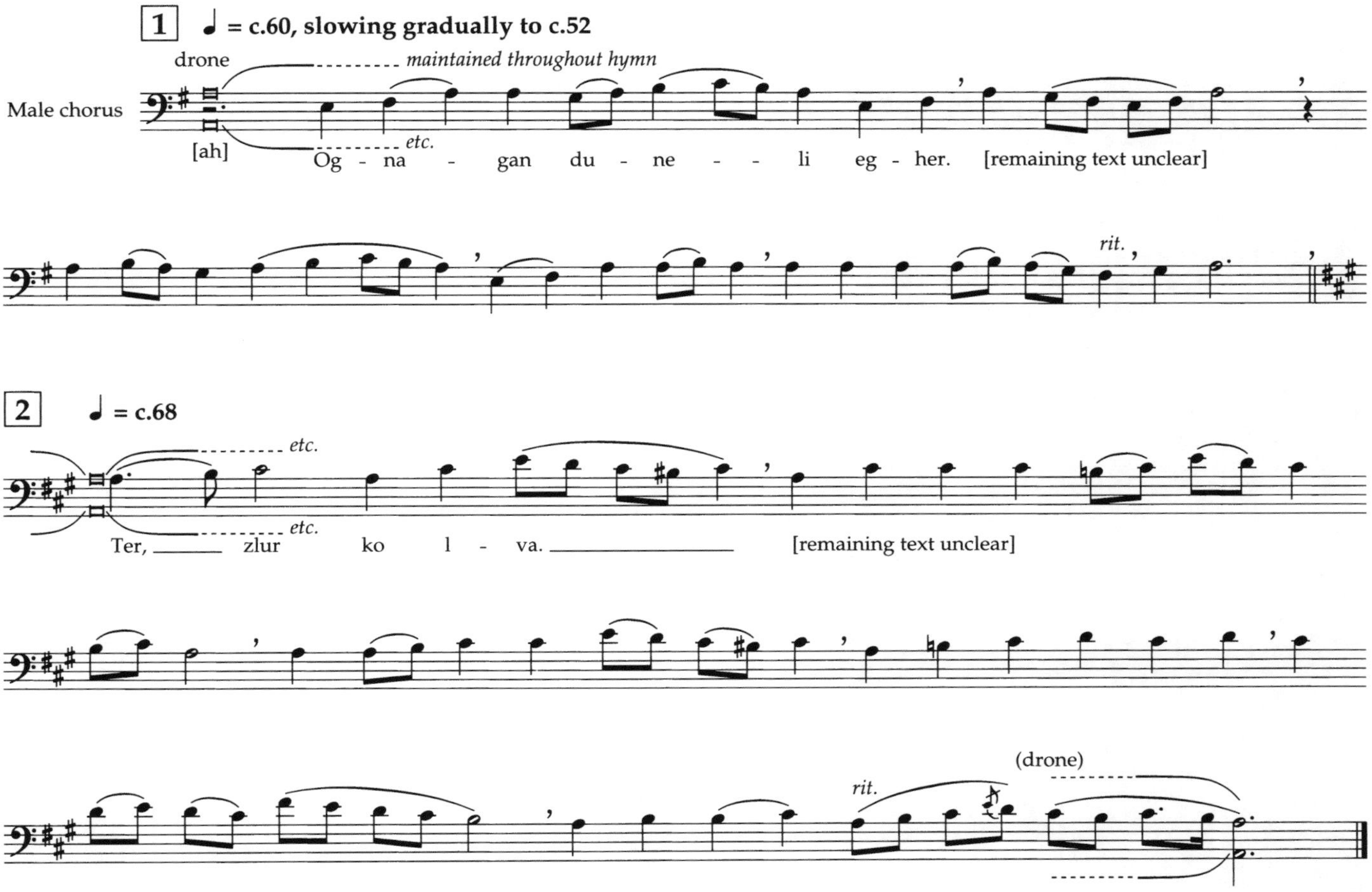
1
♩ = c.60, slowing gradually to c.52
drone
maintained throughout hymn
Male chorus
[ah]
etc.
Og - na - gan du - ne - - li eg - her. [remaining text unclear]
rit.
2
♩ = c.68
etc.
etc.
Ter, zlur ko l - va. [remaining text unclear]
rit.
(drone)

Transcription Notes Vocal drone on pitch A maintained throughout

Opening line of text provided for each section. Remaining phrases unclear

11. Music for *K'amancha*: Life is but a Window

= c.60, but flexible throughout
K'amancha
1.
2.

Transcription Notes

The pitch of some notes is somewhat different from equal-tempered equivalents

The rhythm is flexibly interpreted, with some variation of tempo during and between phrases

↗ slide in direction shown

Georgia

12. Work Song 1: Ourmouli

1
♩ = c.75, but very flexible
Male singer
[text unclear]
2
3
4
5
6

Transcription Notes

The phrase layout is manipulated to make more apparent common features in each phrase

Recorded in a resonant church: the text is difficult to hear clearly and is omitted

Accidentals are effective only within the line in which they appear

↗ vocal slide in direction shown

↑(↓) these pitches are sharper (flatter) than equal-tempered equivalents

13. Work Song 2: Herio da Hopouna

1
♩. = c.56, with acceleration to c.88 by bar 15
Leader
Male chorus
Hey, he - ri-o [song text]
he - ri-o [song text]
etc.
A - hey - hey,
etc.
not quite unison on first note
5
10
15
20
2
[called-out phrase]
... hey.
hey,
call (one voice only)

25
hey, etc.
om etc.
(one voice only)
oy-ya,
om …
ya-ha-ha,

Transcription Notes

Section 2 freer in tempo

Diagonal lines show pitch slides

Song text generally omitted, but repeated vocables shown

Romania

14. Professional Folk Music: Sarpele

1
Taxîm ♩ = c.120
Vioara
Tambal
Contrabas
etc.
5
(tambal continues)
2
Verse 1
1 bar = c.60
10
Voice
(text omitted)
etc. (vioara doubles voice part)
(tambal link)
15
20

25
30
(vioara rests)
35
40
(tambal link)
45
50
vioara joins
(8ve higher and decorated)
55
3 Taxîm
vioara
etc.
(voice rests)

Transcription Notes

Tambal (dulcimer) omitted after first few bars

Vocal text omitted

The barlines in section 1 aid recognition of repeated phrases only; they have no metrical significance

In section 2, time-signatures are employed for convenience alone

∾ ornamentation employed in voice and/or vioara

15. Music for *Cimpoi*: Doina di jele

Cimpoi
♩ = c.58
chanter
middle pipe
drone pipe
(continues throughout)
etc.
etc.

Transcription Notes

The bass drone continues throughout the piece

∾ ornamentation (not transcribed) in melody at this point

Headless notes represent the melody continuing or developing previously transcribed pattern

16. Village Wedding Music: Kalamatianos

♪ = c.252
Clarinet
Lute
Drum
(& B♭ chord)
(F chord)
(tambourine joins in)
5
(lute and tambourine continue)
(drum continues)
10
15
20
25

30
35
40
45
50
55
60
(to A♭)
65
70
(other instruments stop)

Transcription Notes

Only the clarinet part is transcribed throughout; the other parts continue largely as shown at the start

𝆗 untranscribed finger ornament in the clarinet part

Vibrato is used throughout in the clarinet

17. 1930s Folk Dance: Sousta

'hesitant' start
♩ = c.120
Lyra
Laouto
5
10
15
20
25

30
35
40
45
50
laouto continues
55
60
65

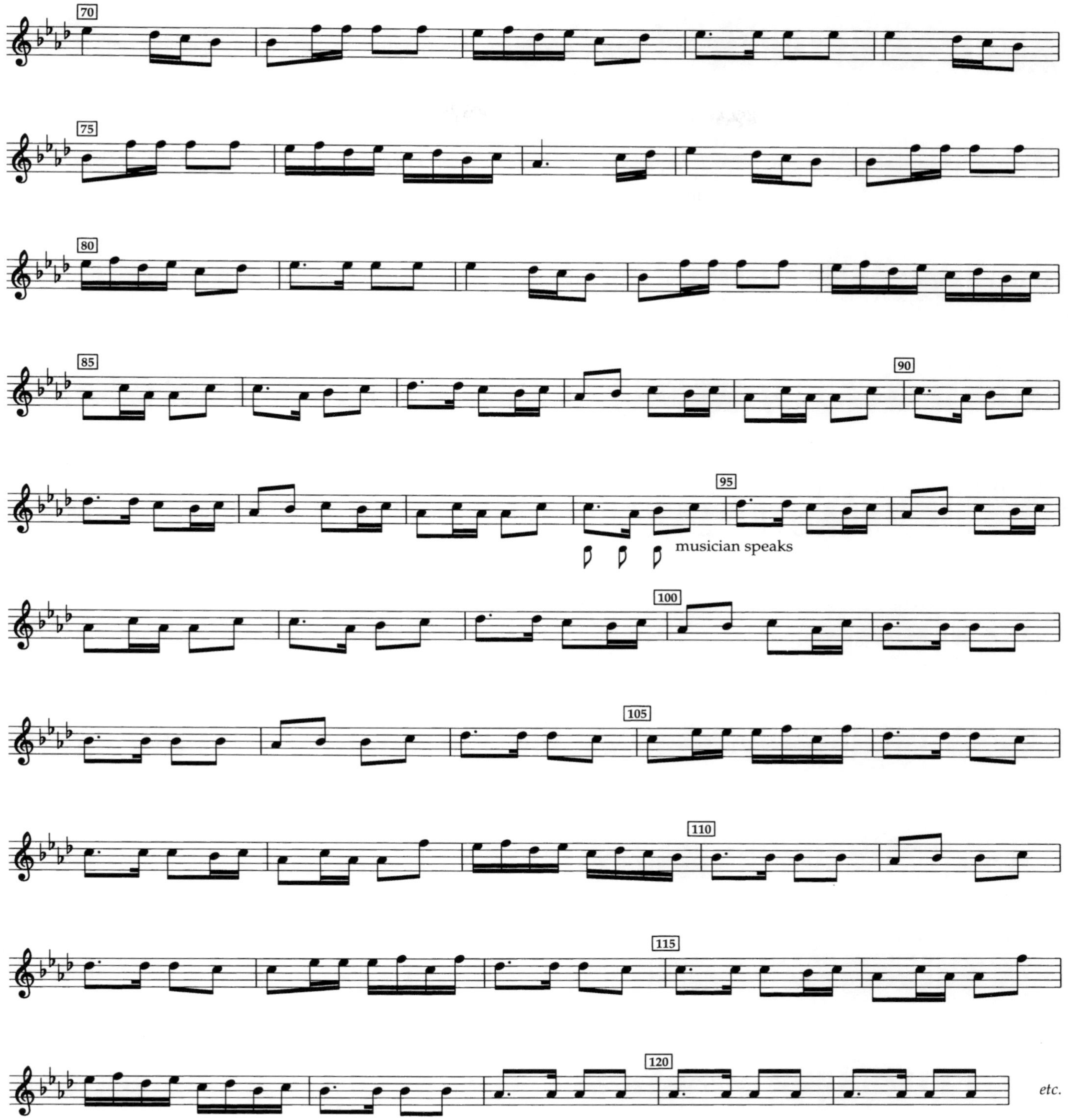
70
75
80
85
90
95
musician speaks
100
105
110
115
120
etc.

Transcription Notes

The laouto continues in similar style throughout

The lyra part shows melodic and rhythmic highlights only (ornamentation omitted)

The lyra typically bows pairs of semiquavers

Occasional intonational discrepancies not marked

18. *Cante Flamenco*: A naí no me gustan las rubias

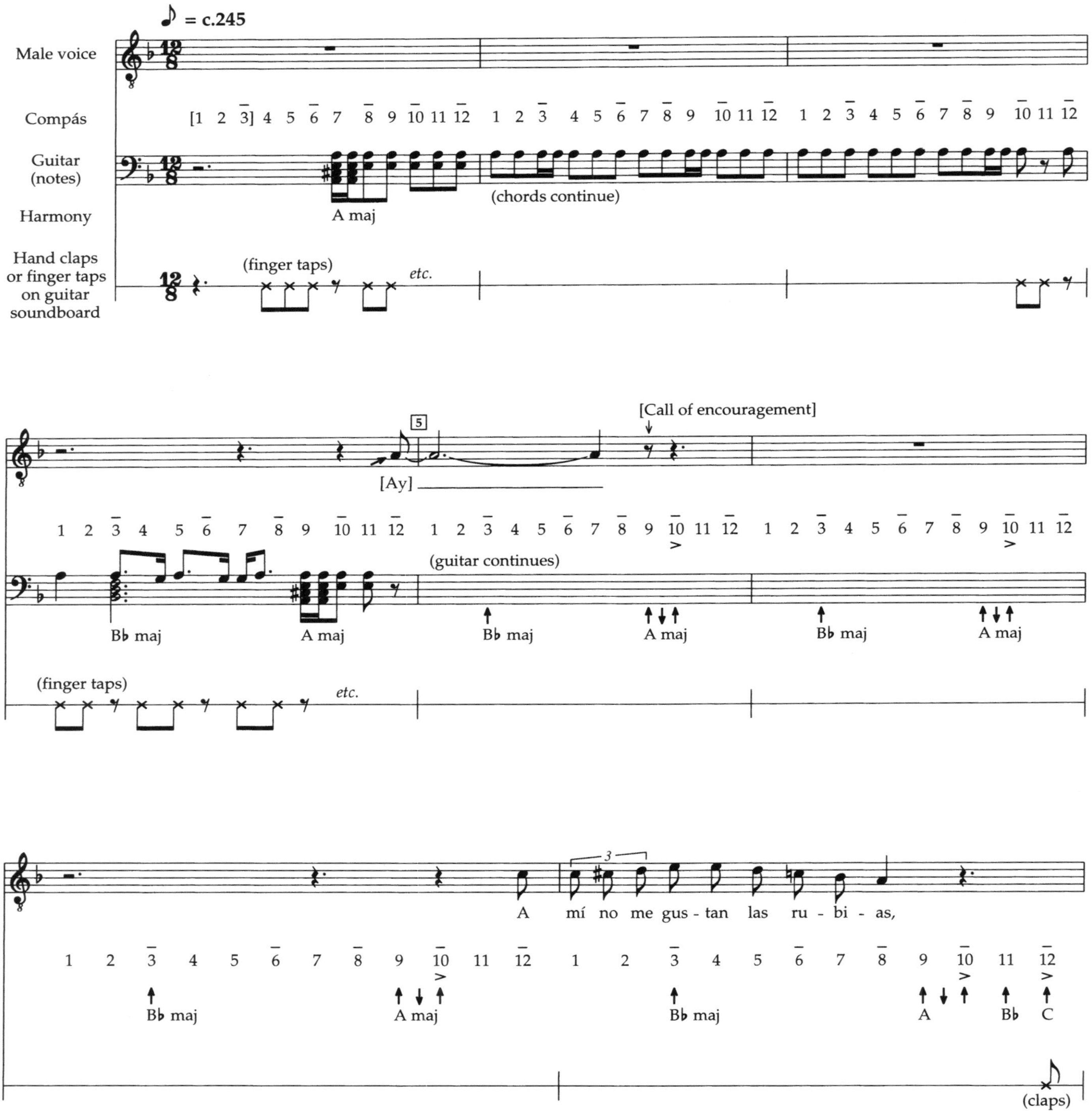

♪ = c.245
Male voice
Compás
Guitar (notes)
Harmony
Hand claps or finger taps on guitar soundboard
(finger taps)
etc.
(chords continue)
A maj
Bb maj
[Call of encouragement]
[Ay]
(guitar continues)
A mí no me gus - tan las ru - bi - as,
A
Bb
C
(claps)

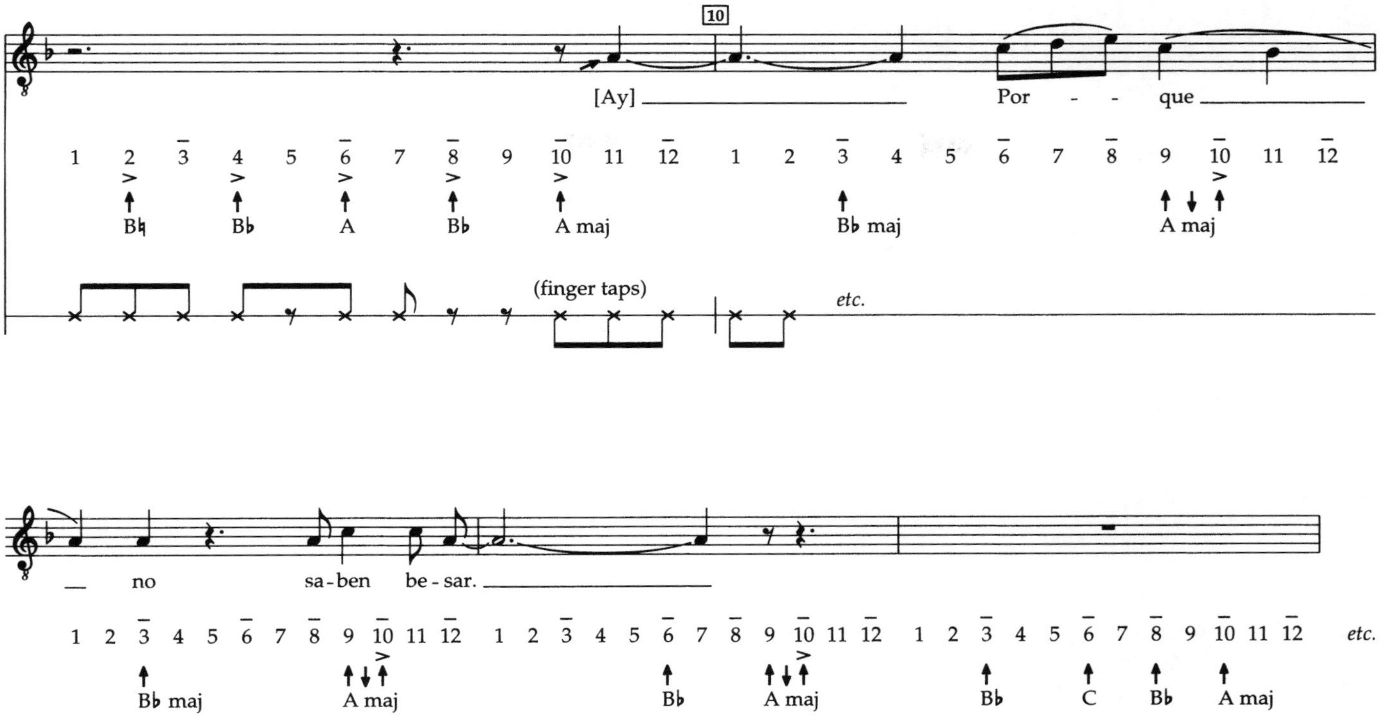
10
[Ay]
Por - - que
1 2 3 4 5 6 7 8 9 10 11 12 1 2 3 4 5 6 7 8 9 10 11 12
B♮ B♭ A B♭ A maj B♭ maj A maj
(finger taps)
etc.
no sa-ben be-sar.
1 2 3 4 5 6 7 8 9 10 11 12 1 2 3 4 5 6 7 8 9 10 11 12 1 2 3 4 5 6 7 8 9 10 11 12
B♭ maj A maj B♭ A maj B♭ C B♭ A maj
etc.

Transcription Notes

Transcribed one semitone above the recorded pitch

Only highlights of the guitar part are shown after the introduction

Compás: rhythmic cycle – principal beats marked

↗ pitch slide in direction shown

↑ B♭ guitar chord

↑↓↑ A maj three repeated guitar chords on the same harmony

Portugal

19. *Fado* Urban Song: Maria Feia

1 Introduction
♩. = c.80
Viola and Guitarra Portuguesa
(bass, harmonies and melodic highlights only)
5
D min [G] C maj D min
C maj D min
10
2 Verse
Voice (one octave lower)
15
Eu não sei co [-mo te] cha-mas, O Ma-ri-a Fei-a,
Cra-vo não que tu és ro-sa,
Nem que no-mo te hei de dôr, O Ma-ri-a Fei-a, O Fei-a Ma-ri-a, O Ma-ri-a Fei-a, O Fei-a Ma-ri-a.
Ro-sa não, que não tem flor,
A maj B♭ maj C maj
20
1st, 3rd, 5th times
F maj A maj D min A maj D min
3 Refrain
2nd, 4th times
-ri-a.
audience hand claps
La, la, la, la, la, la, la.
D min C maj D min

40
La, la, la, la, la, la, la.
C maj
D min

Repeat [2] and [3]

[4] Cadenza and coda

6th time
100
a tempo
- ri - a, O Ma - ri - a Fei - a, O Fei - a Ma - ri - a.
D min
A maj
D min

Transcription Notes

The transcription shows the vocal part (sounding an octave below written pitch) and bass line and melodic passages of accompaniment only. Accompaniment harmonies are outlined below the bass line. Accompaniment melodic passages are enclosed in brackets

The text shown is that for verse 1. In all, there are three verses, two refrains and one final cadenza-coda

Minor variations are found on each repeat

20. Music for *Hardingfele*: Svein I Sy' Garde

♩. = c.58
Hardingfele
Bowed strings
Foot-tapping
etc.
(this pattern repeated throughout)
(re-articulations of same drone string not always shown)

25
2
tr
3
30
35
2
3
40
etc.

Followed by [1] [2] [3] [2] [3] in varied form

Transcription Notes The transcription shows bowed strings only. The foot-beat pattern shown at the beginning continues throughout. Sympathetic strings add extra resonance

↗ slide in direction shown

∾ untranscribed decoration performed on this pitch

21. Lullaby: Bånsull

Verse
♩ = c.108
Female voice
[Text omitted]
5
Refrain
10

Transcription Notes

Text omitted

Key signature adapted to suit the transcription

Extra-beat pauses on final note of verse and refrain are written out with full rhythmic value

Some ♫ rhythm patterns are close to ♪ ♩ (triplet 3)

∾ untranscribed decoration on this pitch

Canada

22. Inuit Throat-Singing: Katajjaq performance

1
♩ = c.110
Voice 1
ha hm ha hm ha hm ha bo-wo-na bi-li-ni bo-wo-na bi-li-ni bo-wo-na
Voice 2
hm ha hm ha hm ha hm ha hm ha hm ha hm
bi-li-ni mi-ne ma-ne mi-ne ma-ne mi-ne ma-ne hm ha hm ha hm ha hm ha
ha hm ha hm ha hm ha hm ha hm ha hm ha hm

2 ♩ = c.60 with gradual acceleration . . . . to ♩ = c.136

(gradually less pitched and more breathy)
(performed 16 times in all)
ha ha ha ha ha ha ha ha ha ha ha ha
hm - ha-ha hm - ha-ha hm - ha-ha hm - ha-ha
ha ha ha ha ha ha ha ha ha ha ha ha
ha-ma-ma ha-ma-ma ha-ma-ma ha-ma-ma

3

♩ = c.60 with acceleration to c.120

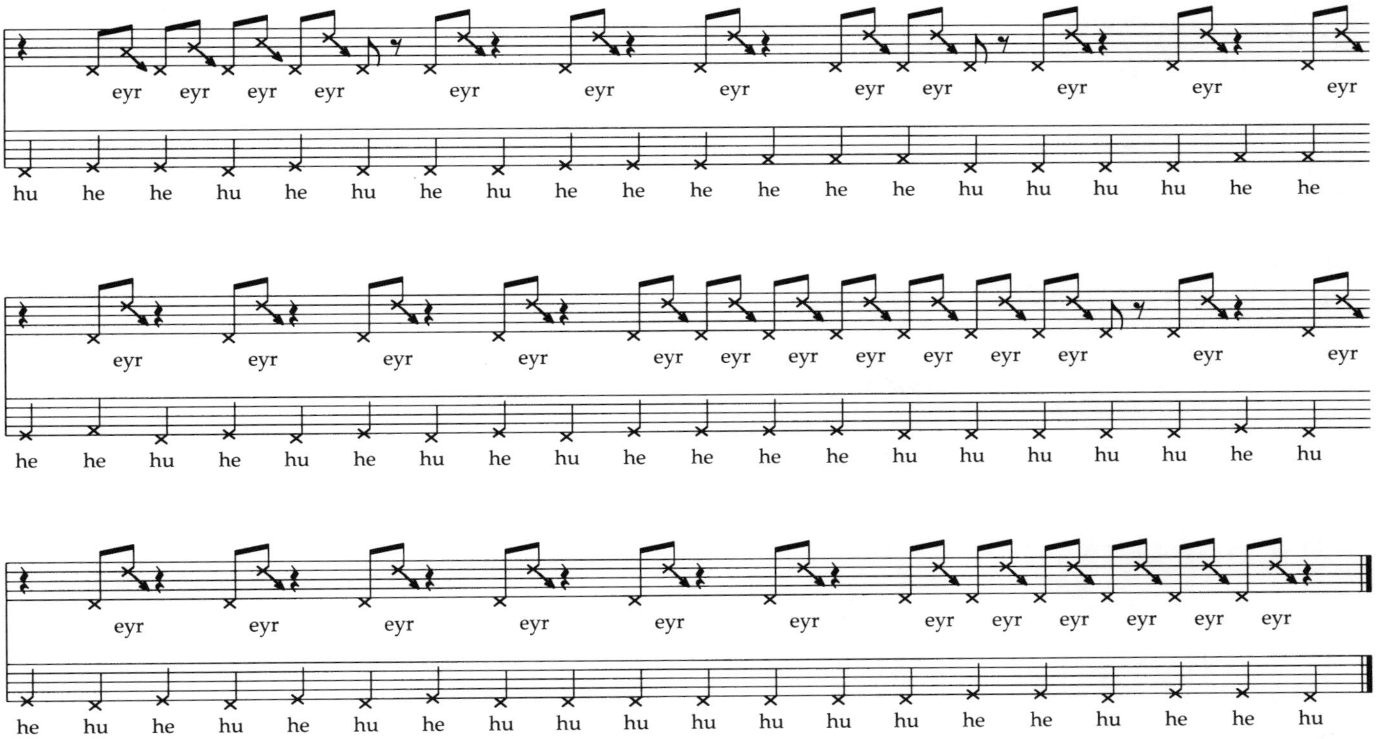
eyr eyr eyr eyr eyr eyr eyr eyr eyr eyr eyr eyr
hu he he hu he hu he hu he he he he he he hu hu hu hu he he
eyr eyr eyr eyr eyr eyr eyr eyr eyr eyr eyr eyr eyr
he he hu he hu he hu he hu he he he he hu hu hu hu hu he hu
eyr eyr eyr eyr eyr eyr eyr eyr eyr eyr eyr eyr
he hu he hu he hu he hu hu hu hu hu hu hu he he hu he he hu

Transcription Notes

Voices keep a moment apart throughout each game, so that the rhythmic patterns overlap; this may not be shown in the transcription

Apart from spoken or sung syllables and sounds (approximately transcribed with letters) rhythmic patterns also include breathing sounds. These have been transcribed only when they can be heard clearly on the recording. When no transcription is given, but a rhythmic value is shown, a panting breath sound is heard

In the third throat-song only approximate relative pitch is shown, not absolute pitch

sound with a more breathy or hummed tone quality

↗ slide in direction shown

23. Inuit Solo Song

1
♩ = c.94
Male voice
Ae yai yai — yai — ya, — Ing mil ai ya en lang a, Ing — mil ai ya — il lang a pi sik
(occasional foot-tapping sound omitted)
2 slight rise in pitch
5
sak si oo long a lu i yai yai yai ya. Ae yai yai — yai — ya, — Pi sik sa ning il luk pung a, —
10
3
Pi — sik sa ning il luk pung a nung oo os si mung ma tae gu ni yai yai ya. Ae yai yai — yai — ya, —
15
Nung oo oo sae ma wa tae gu, Nung moo oo sae ma wa tae gu sae wu dri ta vi sik sa ning i yai yai yai ya.
4
Ae yai yai — yai — ya, — Tai nik sa kai jan ae ra(n), Tai — nik sa kai jan ae ran fae chil
20
5
on na ae kae av tan ae yai yai yai ya. Ae yai yai — yai — ya, — Tai nik sa kai jan ae ra(n),
25
6
Tai — nik sa kai jan ae ran nil jil til jil na dae an nae ni yai yai yai ya. Ae yai yai — yai — ya, —
30
Ka tu ri li va la, Ae — ka tu ri li va la ae jan ot tong nil a oo na ae yai yai yai ya.
etc.

Transcription Notes

The voice rises slightly as it warms up, hence change of key signature

Barlines and beaming are used to highlight phrases and patterns within phrases

↗ ascending pitch slide

Ae vocables

United States of America

24. Sioux Flag Song

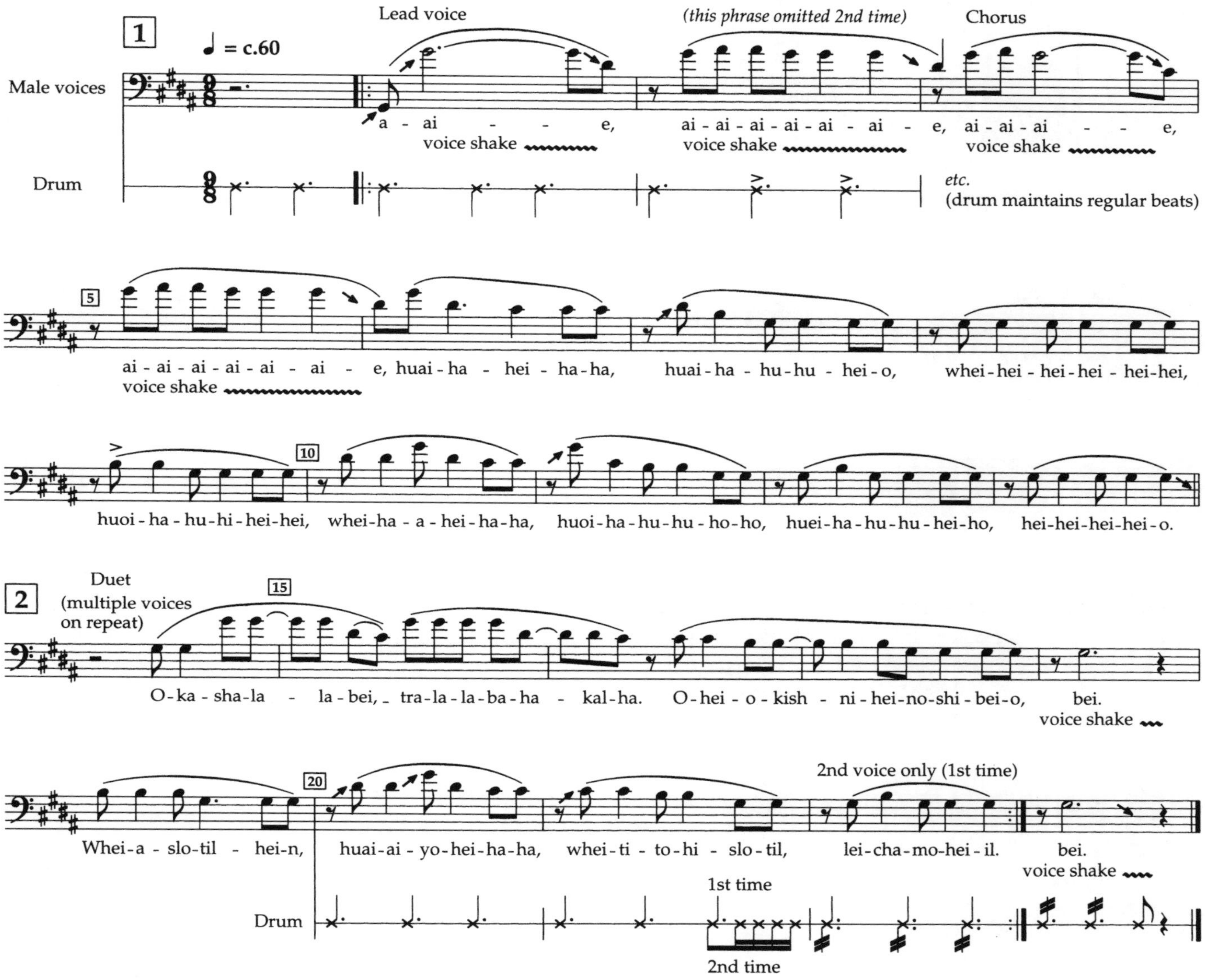
1
♩ = c.60
Male voices
Lead voice
a - ai - - e,
voice shake
(this phrase omitted 2nd time)
ai - ai - ai - ai - ai - ai - e,
voice shake
Chorus
ai - ai - ai - - e,
voice shake
Drum
etc.
(drum maintains regular beats)
5
ai - ai - ai - ai - ai - ai - e, huai - ha - hei - ha-ha,
voice shake
huai - ha - hu-hu - hei - o,
whei-hei - hei-hei - hei-hei,
10
huoi - ha - hu-hi - hei-hei,
whei-ha - a - hei - ha - ha,
huoi-ha - hu - hu - ho-ho,
huei-ha - hu - hu - hei - ho,
hei-hei-hei-hei - o.
2
Duet
(multiple voices
on repeat)
15
O-ka - sha-la - la - bei, tra-la - la-ba-ha - kal-ha.
O-hei - o - kish - ni-hei-no-shi - bei-o,
bei.
voice shake
20
Whei-a - slo-til - hei-n,
huai-ai - yo-hei-ha-ha,
whei-ti - to-hi - slo-til,
2nd voice only (1st time)
lei-cha-mo-hei - il.
bei.
voice shake
Drum
1st time
2nd time

Transcription Notes

In sections of the song for multiple singers, one voice only is transcribed; minor melodic and rhythmic differences in each voice are omitted. Likewise, minor differences during the repeat are not transcribed

Tentative phonetic transcription of Lakota language text:

> consonants as in standard English, vowels: a as 'at', e as 'her', i as 'ee' when completing a syllable but as 'if' when followed by a consonant, o as 'go', u as 'who', composite vowels as these read consecutively

Metrical organization for convenience only

↗ pitch slide in direction marked

The overall song falls slightly in pitch, ending almost a semitone lower than transcribed

25. Texas Folk Song: Godamighty Drag

♩ = c.80 (with gradual increase to c.100)
Male voice
Guitar (bass line and chord symbols)
1. Ma - ma and pa - pa,
2. told me they'd par - don me,
3. June, Ju - ly, Au - gust,
4. Left me here rol - ling,
etc.
Woh Lor - dy!
Ma - ma and
[A] done told me they'd
[A] June, Ju - ly,
[A] left me here
E A E
1. pa - pa, God - a - migh - ty, God knows,
2. par - don me, Oh - ho my Lord,
3. Au - gust, Woh - ho my Lord,
4. rol - ling, Woh - ho my Lord,
etc.
Done told me a lie, sir, Woh
By next Ju - ly, sir, Woh
Done come and gone, sir, Oh
On this old farm, sir, Oh
5
B7 E B7
1. Lor - dy, [A] done told me a lie, sir,
2. Lor - dy, [A] by next Ju - ly, sir,
3. Lor - dy, [A] done come and gone, sir,
4. Lor - dy, On this old farm, sir,
etc.
Woh - ho my Lord.
[2. Done]
B7 A E B7 E

Followed by three more verses, then a return to verses 1 and 2, the final lines of which are hummed rather than sung

Transcription Notes Details of the guitar part are omitted

There are minor melodic and rhythmic differences in each verse

↗ pitch slide in direction indicated

26. Music for Steel Band: Soulful Calypso

1
♩ = c.134
Melodic outline
Lower harmonic line
Harmony:
D
5
21
A
10
26
1.
15
(A)
E min
A7
D
G
D
A
D
etc.
2.
32
2
35
43
D
A
1.
40
2.
50
D
D

Repeat of 1 (from first full bar)

Repeat of 2

Principal percussion:

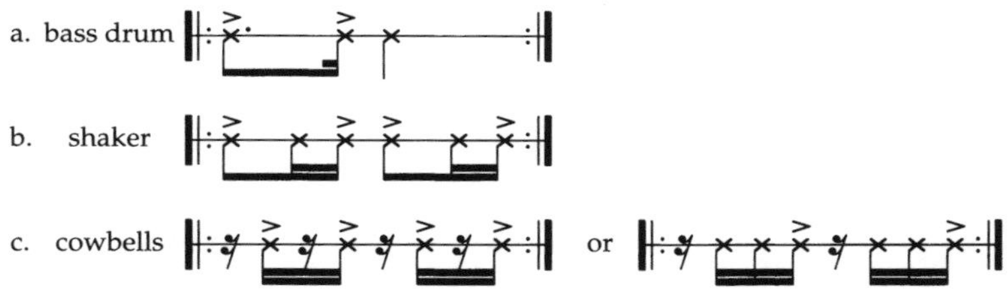
a. bass drum
b. shaker
c. cowbells
or

Transcription Notes

This melodic outline shows the main elements of the upper melody only (one octave below actual pitch)

Basic chord progressions are also shown (D = D major, etc.)

Sample percussion rhythms are shown; these, or variants, continue throughout

Some melodic dotted rhythms are closer to triplet figures

Colombia

27. Dance for *Chirimīa* Ensemble: Viejo Miguel

1
♩ = c.128
A
Chirimías
Percussion omitted
B
5
3
B
10
(♩ = ♩.)
C
C
15
C
C
20
C

2

A twice
B twice
C four times (final bar adapted)

Transcription Notes

Transcribed one semitone below the recorded pitch

To avoid the use of many triplet signs, theme C has been transcribed in $\frac{12}{8}$ metre

Percussion parts, which reiterate the same rhythmic pattern throughout, have been omitted

Four chirimía players perform, mostly in heterophonic parallel thirds. The transcription records the notes heard most distinctly

Repetition of themes A, B and C in section 2 is not exact

28. Kuli Panpipe Ensemble

1
♩ = c.124
Player 1
Player 2
Player 3
5
10
15

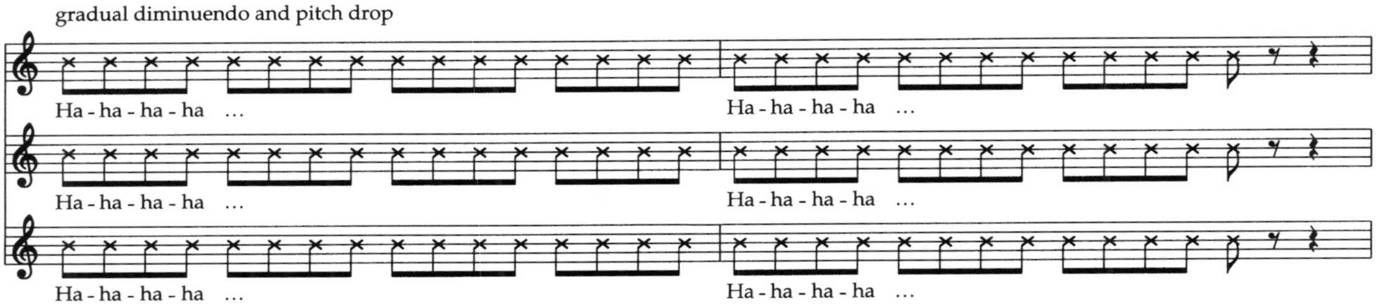
gradual diminuendo and pitch drop
Ha - ha - ha - ha ...
Ha - ha - ha - ha ...
Ha - ha - ha - ha ...
Ha - ha - ha - ha ...
Ha - ha - ha - ha ...
Ha - ha - ha - ha ...

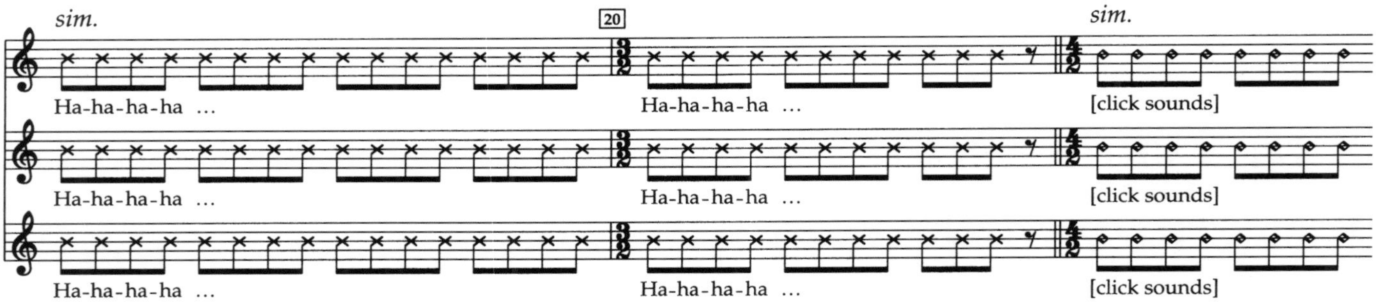
sim.
20
sim.
Ha-ha-ha-ha ...
Ha-ha-ha-ha ...
[click sounds]
Ha-ha-ha-ha ...
Ha-ha-ha-ha ...
[click sounds]
Ha-ha-ha-ha ...
Ha-ha-ha-ha ...
[click sounds]

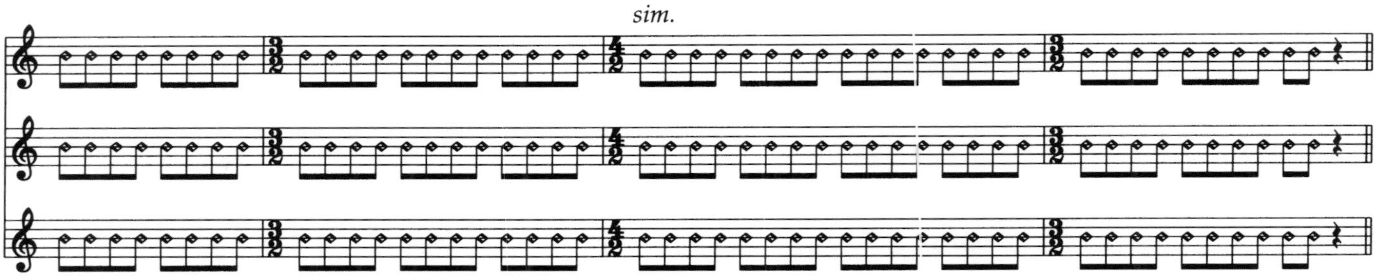
sim.

2 Repeat of bars 1–11

Repeat of bars 12–16, with adapted conclusion

Transcription Notes Intonation is not based on equal-tempered intervals

Repeated passages are modified upon their return

Brazil

29. Ritual Dance-Song Rehearsal: No'ok-'a mor

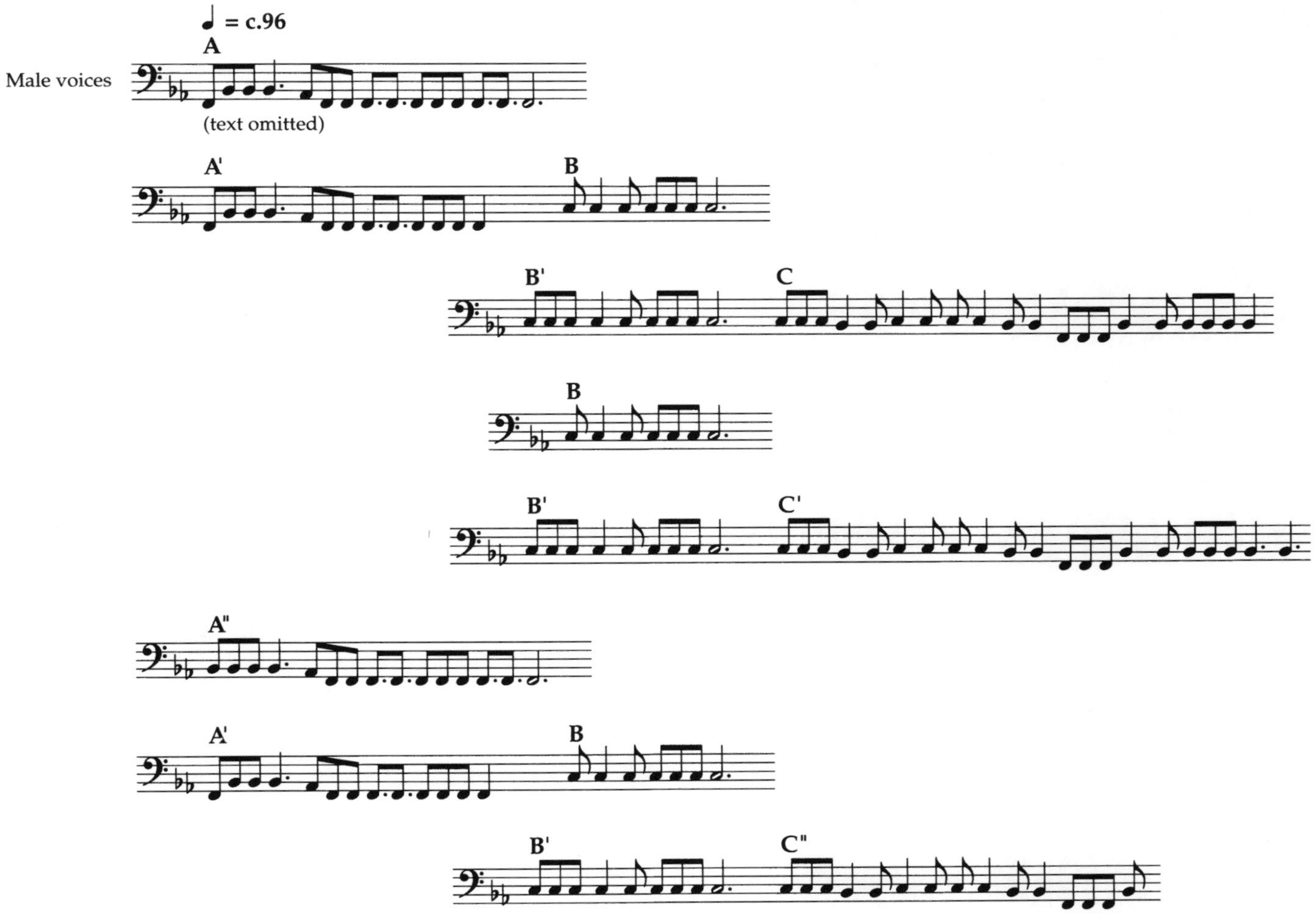

♩ = c.96
A
Male voices
(text omitted)
A'
B
B'
C
B
B'
C'
A"
A'
B
B'
C"

Transcription Notes

Text omitted

The song is sung in unison by adult male voices

The layout of the transcription is manipulated to show phrase structure